THE
LANGUAGE
OF
PATTERN

An enquiry inspired by Islamic decoration

KEITH ALBARN

JENNY MIALL SMITH

STANFORD STEELE

DINAH WALKER

Icon Editions

Harper & Row, Publishers

New York, Evanston, San Francisco,
London

ACKNOWLEDGMENTS

The authors would like to thank the following for their
teaching while working with them on other projects :
Dr James Dickie, Professor Sir Ernst Gombrich,
Professor Richard L. Gregory and Dr Sayyed Hossein
Nasr.
For our introduction to Islam we thank Antony Hutt for
his continued help and encouragement, and Paul Keeler
who, as director, made possible our involvement in the
World of Islam Festival at the Institute of Contemporary
Arts in 1971.
And finally we feel especially indebted to Jo and Ann
Howse for their work on Vedic mathematics, without
which this book would not have been possible.

ERRATA

The publishers regret that the following errors were
noticed in the text too late for alteration.
For 'red' read 'blue' on:
p. 48, col. 1, l. 12
p. 58, l. 7
p. 80, l. 15
p. 90, col. 1, l. 15
p. 92, col. 1, l. 23
p. 98, col. 2, l. 12

FIRST U.S. EDITION

STANDARD BOOK NUMBER : 06-430050-1

LIBRARY OF CONGRESS CATALOG CARD NUMBER :
73-20057

Contents

Foreword

For each of us the known world with its objects, people and spatial relationships is unique, personal and directly experienced. The physical world is inferred from the personal world which represents it. The character and quality of perceptual experience is determined by the nature of the sensory stimuli and the structure and functional capacity of the brain.

Clearly the mind is not a static reflective mechanism which faithfully mirrors external reality or passively distorts the image. Dynamic, vibrant, unique and personal, it moulds conduct, thought and feeling into a life style which orders immediate impressions into patterns and sequences — often in accordance with a pre-conceived or predetermined plan. Scanning the data and ordering it are vital properties of mind.

In this book the fascinating visual patterns excite, each time they are contemplated, new sequences of thought, feeling and urges to action.

But the book contains more than a series of numerically inspired visual patterns. There are tentative yet pertinent comments on the nature and quality of perceptual experience; a plea for wholeness and unity instead of duality and dichotomy; criticism of the disproportionate preoccupation with quantitative rather than qualitative values.

Certainly the undoubted drift towards a technocracy in which the majority are becoming dependent on a minority of specialists and the specialists upon machines more complex than the data they deal with, is contrary to the Western way of life in the sense that the people are non-participants in the events which control their destinies.

This book with its geometric patterns and visual communications somehow cuts through the confusing values of contemporary social organization and exposes the primary data of unity, order and evolution.

London, 1973   G. D. FRASER STEELE

Introduction

We were inspired to the study which produced this book by the art of Islam. As Western designers we had learnt to regard pattern as superficial decoration of form, and form as dictated by function. But here was an art and architecture concerned with illusion as much as function, emblazoned with dynamic interlacings of pattern and script.

Yet it was apparent that this richness of invention was based on order, and represented a blend of the organic and geometric; a synthesis of objective and subjective understanding of nature.

In order to deepen our experience and understanding of Islamic art, we set out to discover the methods (and in the process the motivations) of the original designers. In reworking this material we began to understand the nature and the role of a visual language.

The reader can follow our processes and their implications in the following chapters. Our first reading of the concepts embodied in Islamic pattern was confirmed by what we later learned of Islamic culture, touched on in Chapter 4.

The ability to perceive pattern and make connections, to see parts in relation to the whole, is vital to us in the West where a culture based on dichotomy (art-science, material-spiritual, etc.) has been led by a rapidly developing technology towards excessive analysis at the expense of synthesis.

1 Number and Pattern

In fig. 1 of the diagram opposite we see an array of dots. The first six patterns of these dots remind us of dominoes, each with a specific quantity of dots which evokes a memory of a numeral.

The dots are not seen merely as discs of black ink on a white paper surface to be counted, but as significant patterns acting like hieroglyphics, a convention of notation which we expect others will read in a similar way. We recognize that an established system is at work.

Such a system's notation, developed from the hieroglyphics and other materials available at any particular time, can either facilitate or hinder its development (e.g. Roman numerals are cumbersome in multiplication) and, even more importantly, influence or even determine the ideas which are generated by the system in use. Obviously, if a system is to be successfully developed we must employ both suitable processes and well-adapted visual forms. And in order to allow us to extend our sphere of operation, we must help our memories by externalizing our concepts (in the context of these diagrams, the concepts generated by counting).

Counting is one of many factors in our building up of an 'internal model' of the perceived world. The marks we make (such as the dominoes) are an 'externalization' of our internal model; and the very process of making these patterns, an 'external model', will in turn modify our perception of the external world.

This interaction between the internal and the external can continue indefinitely and generate fresh perceptions and conceptions as it goes along, without reference to the original stimulus. New ideas are generated to be tested in the 'real' world.

We count real things, but what if those things should disappear, would that mean the end of counting?

In the beginning there was not 'nothing'.

Nothing did not exist.

No thing did not exist.

There was emptiness and absence.

But as the internal model is developed its dependence on the real world is seemingly lessened, or the ambiguous nature of perception is recognized. Then it is possible to contemplate that: nothing is real; nothing exists.

It was partly this ambiguity of language which allowed for the emergence of the idea of zero. Zero as a concept is the internal model of a sophisticated mind. Because of its infinite nature it immediately encourages the drive to order and cross-reference, and thus creates new concepts.

It is as difficult to conceive of zero dimensions as it is to conceive of the fourth dimension. In a zero-dimensional world there is no perception – zero as a concept is independent of the external world; but armed with its implications we can make great strides in ordering our models of that world.

The zero has to have a mark to notate its existence, and we use the circle or dot. Its ambiguities are legion; for instance if we can imagine the page white on black, a switch from positive to negative, then the perceptual process suggests a hole in the black sheet of paper or a star in the night sky (of indeterminate size and distance). A hole implies a delimiting surface or solid; it is a negative dot. Or to extend the implications, we see in punch-card data stores holes (negative zero dimensions) in surface (2D) with rods (one dimension) creating banks (3D) of information, implying a further extension into a fourth dimension.

A more direct example of the exploration of a visual-conceptual idea is the artist's use of short tentative lines or dots as an illusionary device, preventing a too firm commitment to the developing idea and allowing the page to speak back to him.

But the ordering drive is such that the brain will always attempt to 'see' a pattern. The groups of dots illustrated (figs. 7–12 opposite) reveal *after* construction new facts about numbers and relationships of numerals in serial form. Similar games can be played in three dimensions, using pyramids of pebbles etc. to develop tetrahedral series of numbers, subject only to the physical limitations of size.

These processes show us that a wealth of information can be stored within a simple pattern. Hence the significance to us of such patterns, still felt intuitively long after the original function has fallen into disuse.

We are now so used to and dependent upon the purely counting function of the numeral that we rarely question its nature either as a visual element or as a stimulus for recalling anything other than a specific quantity (and even the latter is often not consciously considered).

In earlier times, when the technical extensors of memory such as computers were fewer, and the concepts of number and numeral were fresher in the mind of man, number patterns were keys to a whole cultural ethos, an expression of man's relationship to the universe. In the early art of Islam, for instance, concept, number, and pattern were closely interrelated, and by cross-reference aided one another's development.

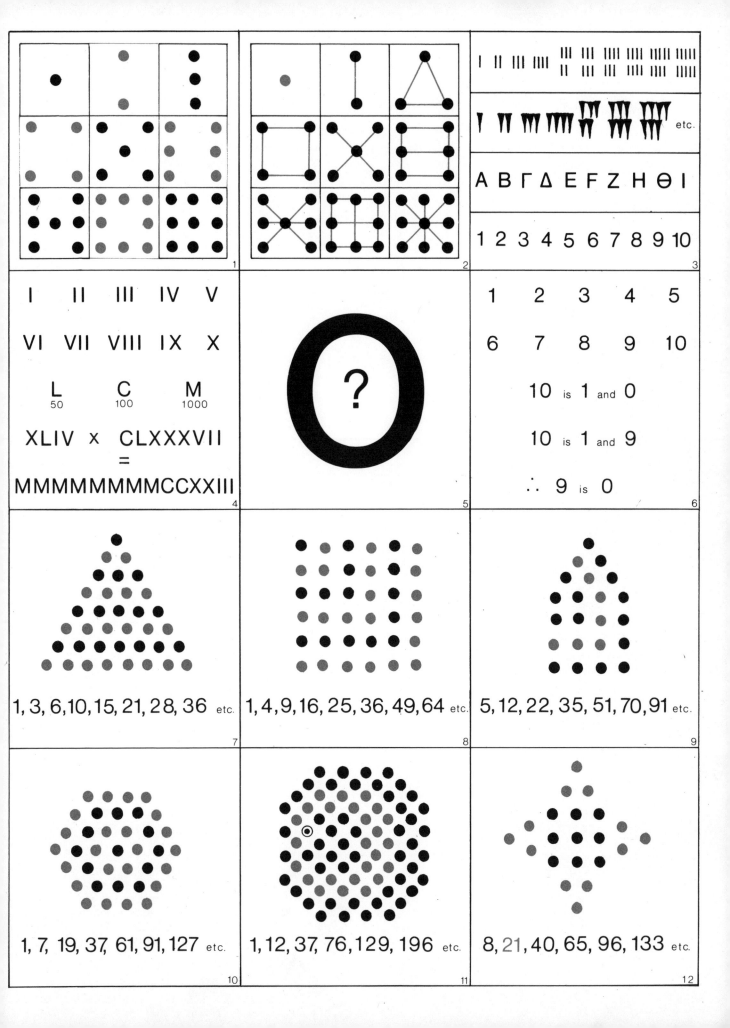

1

2

3

I	II	III	IV	V
VI	VII	VIII	IX	X

L C M
50 100 1000

XLIV × CLXXXVII
=
MMMMMMMMCCXXIII

4

?

5

1	2	3	4	5
6	7	8	9	10

10 is 1 and 0

10 is 1 and 9

∴ 9 is 0

6

1, 3, 6, 10, 15, 21, 28, 36 etc.

7

1, 4, 9, 16, 25, 36, 49, 64 etc.

8

5, 12, 22, 35, 51, 70, 91 etc.

9

1, 7, 19, 37, 61, 91, 127 etc.

10

1, 12, 37, 76, 129, 196 etc.

11

8, 21, 40, 65, 96, 133 etc.

12

One pattern of numbers that has held great significance in the past is the multiplication square illustrated opposite (fig. 3). This is known as the Vedic square, and was the basis of a whole mathematical system which contained a numerical model of the universe. In AD 770 the Muslims integrated this North Indian system into their own synthesis of ancient systems.

The square is formed on a nine-by-nine grid numbered one to nine horizontally and vertically from the top left-hand corner. At the intersection of each of the vertical and horizontal columns is the product of the two numbers. When the product exceeds nine the two digits are added together to form a simple digit (fig. 2), and the grid is filled. As we shall see, this cabbalistic reduction of numbers larger than nine has many uses.

When we look at the completed square we are aware of numerical relationships revealing characteristic visual patterns; each number, line of numbers, or interconnection of like numbers has a specific form. Crucial to the understanding of the square is the recognition of the reflection of one and eight, two and seven, three and six, four and five, all pairs which added together equal the remaining number, nine. Each vertical column of numbers has its identical partner in the horizontal column. Like numbers once joined (figs. 4–11) reveal a similar pattern of reflection, and furthermore these figures enclose a group of numbers which when added up can be reduced (by cabbalistic reduction) to that figure (excepting two and seven, whose enclosed squares total twice the figure). The reflecting numbers have a unique character. The two and seven also form the centre of the one to eight square, and total, after reduction, nine.

Seven is the centre of the Vedic square, which may indicate the origin of its magical importance. (Seven is said to be the most commonly chosen number if a subject is requested to name a number lower than nine, possibly an echo of its one-time significance.) Two, of course, is the dual of seven. It is interesting to note that seven and two form the angle of the pentagon; twenty degrees is the angle of a double nonagon; a figure squared employs a two; the diagonal of the square is equal to the long side of a root-two rectangle, with the side of the square as the shorter side; twenty-two over seven is pi.

1	2	3	4	5	6	7	8	9
2	4	6	8					
3	6	9						
4	8							
5								
6								
7								
8								
9								

$$2 \times 5 = 10$$
$$1 + 0 = 1$$

$$7 \times 8 = 56$$
$$5 + 6 = 11$$
$$1 + 1 = 2$$

1	2	3	4	5	6	7	8	9
2	4	6	8	1	3	5	7	9
3	6	9	3	6	9	3	6	9
4	8	3	7	2	6	1	5	9
5	1	6	2	7	3	8	4	9
6	3	9	6	3	9	6	3	9
7	5	3	1	8	6	4	2	9
8	7	6	5	4	3	2	1	9
9	9	9	9	9	9	9	9	9

In figs. 1–5 opposite we can follow the concentric ring of squares that structure the Vedic square, noting that each ring, after reduction, adds up to nine. In fig. 6 the two diagonals of the square contain, in addition to nine, one, four, and seven in one direction, and two, five, and eight in the other. These numbers have considerable significance in the inner structure of numerals (see page 33).

The numerals one to nine are applied to a circle and interconnected in pairs of reflecting numbers (figs. 7–12). The odd number is always half the sum of the joined pairs except for nine, when it is equal to the sum of the pairs. The final figure in the diagram on page 13 is the superimposition of those connections, forming a nest of nonagonal stars. (Note: nine muses; nine-day wonder; ninepins; nine-men's morris; nine lives of the cat.) This square contains much more information than we have space to describe here. Undoubtedly the initial construction of the square led directly to many of the later concepts by feeding back new information to the builder.

So mathematics has grown from continual externalization. It developed through use, in processes not necessarily of application, often merely during manipulation of its own proliferating systems (maths for maths' sake) and in the recording of those sequences. Notation has had to become ever faster and more efficient, until the process of calculation (its application) was removed from man to his extensor, the computer. The theoretical development can and does continue, even seemingly divorced from its application, as long as somewhere within the whole discipline the stimulus of application still occurs.

Throughout the history of ideas we find constant reference to mathematics as an aesthetic; to the recognition of fundamental orders, sequences and patterns. Music, painting and poetry are all means of relating the internal and external models of reality.

On the page opposite we have progressed from the dot to joining points by lines. This use of line on the two-dimensional surface is an extension of our vocabulary of illusion. The ambiguity of line on a two-dimensional surface is very apparent, but we tend to accept the convention of the symbols composed of line, even when the positive line becomes a negative line or groove. We are not always aware of the extent to which the eye is deceived by line in two or three dimensions. A line divorced from its page is one-dimensional; it can be seen as the trace of a dot in time, implying that it has a dot of zero as its cross-section. An imaginary one-dimensional being would only be able to see his line as the dot of a cross-section.

Phrases such as 'lines of communication' reveal the way we now read line as synonymous with energy, i.e. having a dynamic. Interconnect points, and the units thus interconnected become points in triangular relationships, grids, nets, and so on. Dual relationships imply balance, tension, bond and possible isolation. Other configurations will similarly suggest relationships of a wider kind, involving our experiences and feelings. Pattern in a simple context can help us to represent to ourselves our real-life relationships and experiences. It follows that if we increase our ability to see patterns as models, then we should be better able to understand and cross-relate real-life situations.

'Transformation' is the term we use in this book for the process by which we transpose a pattern creatively from one context to another, making use of changes of scale, dimension and viewpoint to trigger off fresh perceptions.

If we turn again to the Vedic square (page 11) we immediately see a mass of numbers and attend to the notation; but our internal model-making requires that we order, so we begin the selection of useful clues. The dominant patterns attract attention like brighter lights. Scanning the square we see numbers repeated. We pick out the like numbers, e.g. two, and tend to group them into a unit; our attention is directed towards selecting pattern through numbers. Seven and two are adjacent numbers, so we now see a small enclosed figure of sevens and twos in the centre of the square. This focus is reinforced by the symmetry of the square and our need to order. If we next see nine, three, six, nine, we see a square pattern enclosing and surrounded by space. A repetitive pattern of nines will result in a larger square enclosing space. If we attend again to the shape of the square, the most prominent features are its corners. Attention is then in a diagonal direction and reveals a number sequence. From this attention we have learned the reflective properties of this square.

Thus from a simple 'whole' we have been able to abstract concepts of like numbers, enclosure, pairs, concentricity, reflecting symmetry and repeats. At a later stage and with more knowledge of the square we could superimpose the double patterns of reflecting numbers to form numerous cross-patterns. This ability to illuminate parts is of the greatest importance, as the parts can then be reorganized to form new relationships.

Alternation of attention between objects is the basis of many illusions. Looking at a projection of a cube in line (page 105), we see it turn in and out, offering two possible interpretations. Our attention oscillates between the two, so that its duration is increased. This particular ambiguity (which depends on our knowledge of cubes) and similar perceptual phenomena can be used consciously as a tool in exploring visual ideas, and in parallel, ideas of wider and more profound significance — as in Islamic decorative patterns, where as we shall see in Chapter 2, illusionary constructions are used to express concepts of mobility and transience.

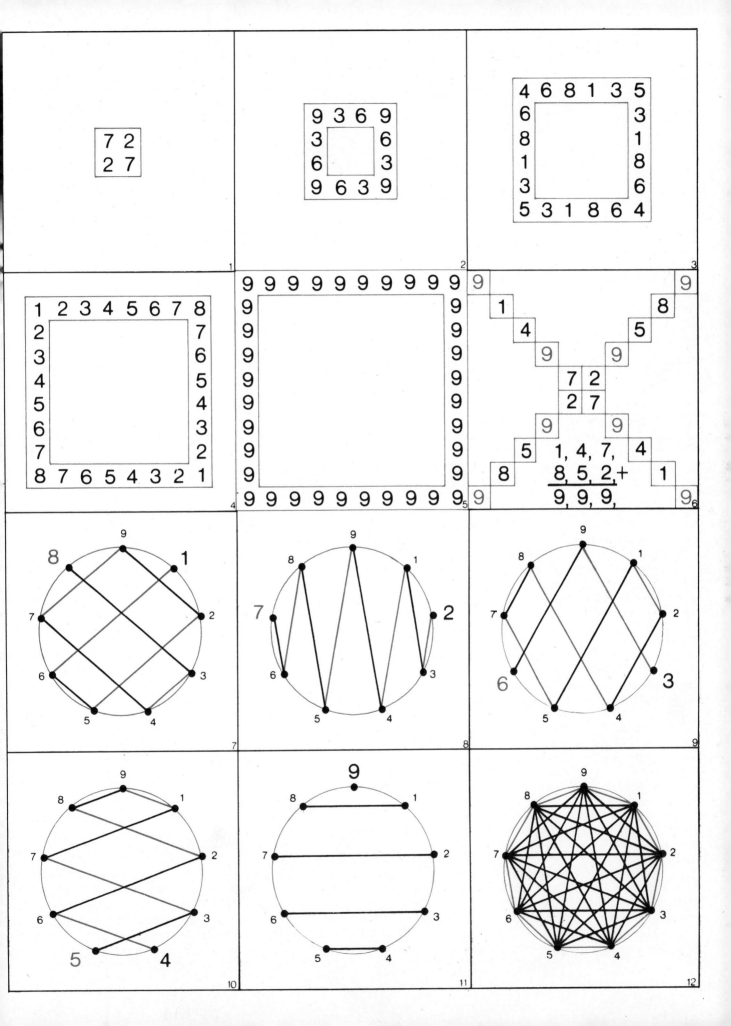

Illustrated on the previous page were the concentric rings of the Vedic square. Opposite, we examine the behaviour of expanding rings of squares numbered according to the stage of growth reached from the centre (one). The squares generate a series of numbers — one followed by eight twos, and so on. At each stage we add the total number of squares so at stage two there are nine squares, at stage three there are twenty-five squares, and so on. The number series is then reduced as previously explained (twenty-five becomes seven). This series is plotted as a graph (fig. 2) whose coordinates are nought to nine and nought to eighteen (or nine when reduced). The number series is obviously a series of square numbers with a distinctive rhythm demonstrated numerically and by the graph. Without cabbalistic reduction such progressions would not be feasible in graph form, so that the pattern would not always appear. Throughout the book we have used the reduction method to study the nature of processes, serial events and structures. Only with this method are certain relationships made evident; i.e. a series of adjacent square numbers (wherever you may start) will always form this rhythm and the relevance of one, four, seven, nine, in the structure of numbers is further understood (see page 33).

The concentric development of close-packed hexagons reveals a distinctive number series of ones and sevens with a specific rhythm expressed more economically than on page 9, fig. 10.

These two configurations representing two elementary nets, grids, or plan views of structures employ the square and the hexagon; shapes with very different characteristics, though both are basic modular units. The square develops continual straight-line sliding divisions in its net both vertically and horizontally and is therefore unstable, while the hexagon locks together without such divisions and is structurally firmer. However, the square grid repeats the square proportionately, and in concentric development is always a perfect mimic of its modular unit, whereas the hexagonal grid, though approximating the basic unit, has castellated edges (fig. 8). (Modular units are much in evidence in modern construction, and we hope to demonstrate that they are fundamental to our artifacts; with our present highly-developed technical facilities we should be able to exploit our processes to match our concepts, and vice-versa.)

As the moving point leaves a trace we call a line, so the moving line leaves a trace we call a plane. The nature of the plane is determined primarily by its line cross-section. So a straight line leaves a flat plane, an 'unstraight' line an 'unflat' plane. The imaginary inhabitants of a two-dimensional world will see only line; the objects passing through their world will only be seen as their cross-sections edge on; i.e., the position of the viewer is critical to his deduction of the nature of any phenomenon. If a tube were to penetrate a two-dimensional world we would only be able to determine its circular shape by travelling round the edge. If a cone were slowly to penetrate a flat world we would notice a dot which gradually increased in size, displacing more and more two-dimensional space, and we would require more and more time to circumnavigate it in order to build up our internal model of it.

The relationship of zero, one and two dimensions is that from each the viewer sees only the previous dimension. We depend on time, movement and multiple views to comprehend the phenomena of the real world.

The line patterns opposite are constructed of *one*-dimensional elements to form on a *two*-dimensional surface an illusion of *three* dimensions. The square grid, if we are aware of the practice of plan projection, can reasonably easily be imagined as a plan drawing of a ziggarat, or a stepped hole with a square at the bottom. The hexagonal grid is much more stubborn. In a single line square the concentration of vision is held within the boundaries of the square, and the contained area of square can appear whiter than the remainder of the page. If two concentric squares are drawn, they are seen as a frame and the surface of the paper is no longer consciously considered. If more than two concentric squares are used then a tunnel effect is produced.

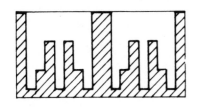

197494791 197494791

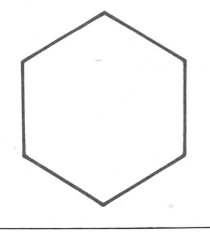

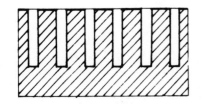

1711711171 171171171

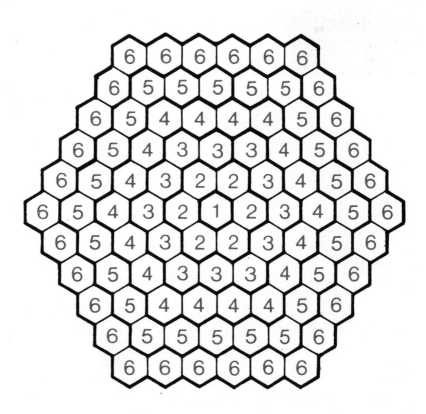

In fig. 4 we see again that the square-based net is the most illusionary, here resembling seven vertical bars laid upon seven horizontal bars. The illusionary vocabulary of square forms is dealt with more fully later on, and it is sufficient to say here that in its familiar axis the square appears to be stable — it encloses and is introspective. On a diagonal axis its character is altered — it implies instability and is therefore more open to development. We see in the square the potential for either balance or imbalance. The hexagon is less ambiguous and is expansive in character, yet it combines the 'feeling' of square and triangle.

The open lattice illustrated in fig. 4 opposite has been constructed according to a simple rule: that is, at each stage only one face of a new square shall touch the faces of another square. At each stage, the total number of squares is counted; this, when transformed into number series and graph, reveals a complex irregular sequence with no apparent order. But, as is so often the case, further reduction or transformations will reveal the underlying rhythm.

If one extracts from the first few numbers only alternate numbers then a series is seen, instantly recognizable as being the same as the previous square rhythm — that of one, nine, seven, four. However after the first eight numbers it breaks down. If one reduces this series again one finds that eventually the rhythm becomes apparent (using one, four, seven, nought; see page 33).

The hexagonal growth with a similar governor (i.e. using similar rules) illustrates by simple reduction the formation of a nucleus necessary before the rhythm of development can begin; once that nucleus is established the rhythm is maintained into infinity. This analogy to the fundamental patterns of growth is in contrast with the modular close-packing development illustrated on the previous page. The most elegant example of such a system generating enormous richness and diversity is the snowflake.

The reader can repeat this game with multi-axial forms of his choice, observing the subtle variations of form, re-ordered and extended in the growing numerical sequences and graphs.

We fear chaos — or perhaps our real fear is of the breakdown of the ordering capacity in our own internal model. As long as our internal model is 'convincing', i.e. well structured, then we will be undeterred by meeting apparent chaos — indeed be greedy for new and disordered material. Patterns are necessary, but they must be seen as open-ended or capable of transformation to keep our concepts developing. It is the methods developed to sustain the movement that are crucial in creative thinking.

Growth of ideas, like growth in nature, is based upon fundamental patterns, continually stimulated by external forces and maintaining an unstable symmetry.

1

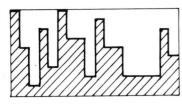

2

15937144 82558888 etc

3

	7		5		3		8		3		5		7	
7		7	6	7		8	7	8		7	6	7		7
	7		7		8		6		8		7		7	
5	6	7		8	7	6	5	6	7	8		7	6	5
	7		8		8		4		8		8		7	
3		8	7	8		4	3	4		8	7	8		3
	8		6		4		2		4		6		8	
8	7	6	5	4	3	2	1	2	3	4	5	6	7	8
	8		6		4		2		4		6		8	
3		8	7	8		4	3	4		8	7	8		3
	7		8		8		4		8		8		7	
5	6	7		8	7	6	5	6	7	8		7	6	5
	7		7		8		6		8		7		7	
7		7	6	7		8	7	8		7	6	7		7
	7		5		3		8		3		5		7	

4

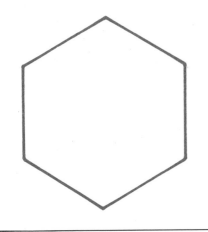

5

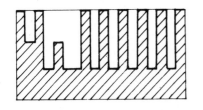

6

14174771717171 71 etc

7

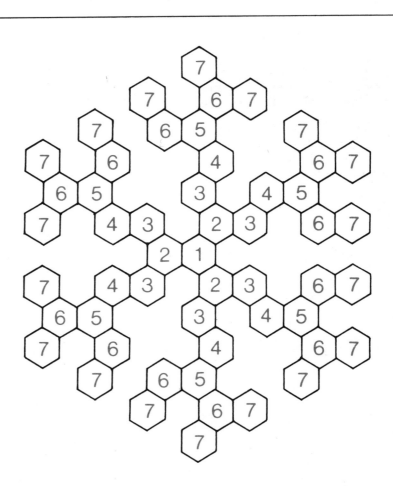

The patterns in the figures on page 15 were close-packing squares and hexagons — the basis of the most simple grids or nets — followed by growth lattices of the same two polygons (page 17). On the facing page we have chosen one of many possible ways of developing nets of polygons which have an odd number of sides, using the pentagon and heptagon. The method of development is again concentric.

The pentagonal net generated by this method clearly demonstrates a regular rhythm within these odd polygons. Off each side of the first pentagon we can see a one, two, two, one growth. This will repeat in an infinite cycle of concentric development. By joining the centres of the pentagon we generate a sub-net which is a close-packing of rectangles and triangles. These rectangles and triangles reveal a mathematical ratio of root-three as a system of proportion (the ratio of the sides of a rectangle formed by enclosing our equilateral triangle). However, the pattern most commonly associated with the pentagon is the pentacle, which contains the Golden Mean ratio.

The heptagon is visually more complex but the same development is seen to operate, although with the addition of overlap. The sub-net reveals a similar arrangement of rectangles and triangles. The order within this net is the Golden Mean, which is usually associated with the previous figure. In rectilinear form this appears in architecture from the Greeks onward, and is also found as a logarithmic spiral in natural forms.

The last odd polygonal net illustrated is the nonagonal develop-ment (page 21, fig. 3). This net reveals the root-two as a proportional system within the sub-net. (The root-two ratio is the side of a square to its diagonal.) The square and octagon are fundamental forms which have been given symbolic significance in almost all cultures.

These relationships between net and sub-net demonstrate the evolution of one order from another, and the interrelationship between the systems, which could now self-generate without further cross-reference. This layering, derived from ordering the external model, multiplies the levels of possible developments. It makes easier the drawing of complex polygonal nets, opens up possibilities of extending the vocabulary of pattern by playing with the resulting elements (figs. 2, 3, 5, 6), and allows prediction of the ordering of more complex situations. In other words, we can now expect more complex even polygons to generate triangular sub-nets, while odd polygonal nets will generate mixed sub-nets of triangles and rectangles. Thus the odd, though less easily ordered, offers the greatest number of possibilities. It appears that in operating repetitive units or modules, we are not merely being perverse if we disguise their origins and create ambiguity, since by doing so we hold the viewer's attention and encourage him to extend his model-making.

We shall see that in Islamic decoration the regular grids are disguised by the layered development of the pattern, and in addition, the patterns imply complex closed grids of even and odd polygons as sub-nets.

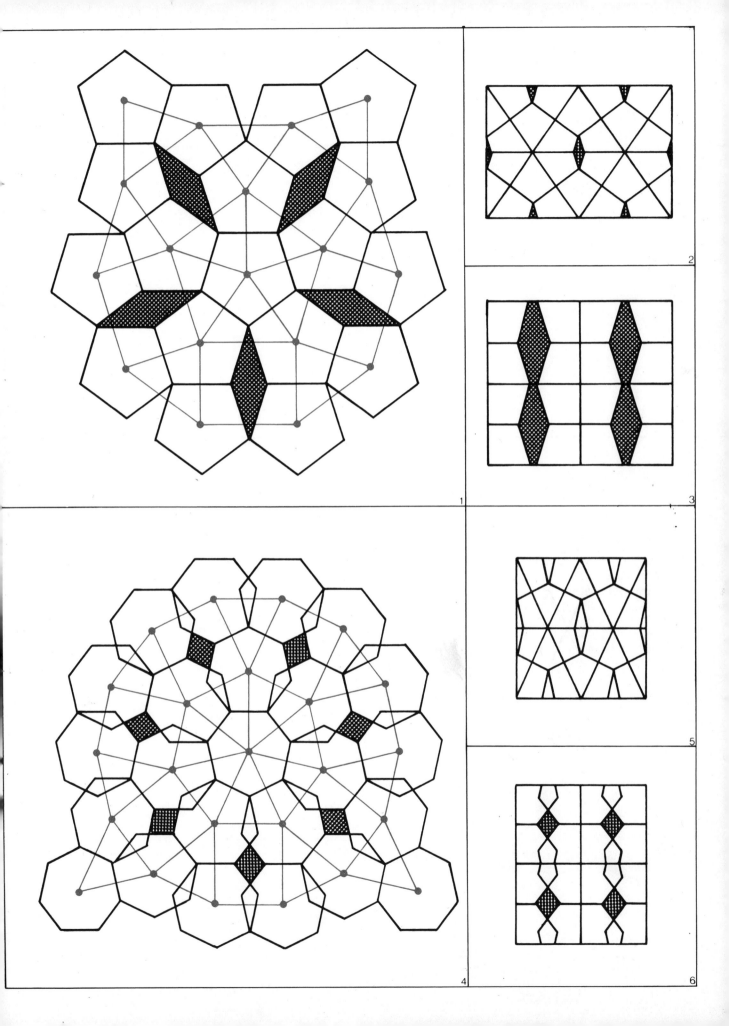

Our attitudes and aims, personal and cultural, determine our response to data from within and without. These data are of relationships or whole configurations, at first blurred, that we organize to form meaningful and significant patterns. Pattern is qualitative, the whole possessing characteristics not owned by the parts.

Analyses of parts, their character and position in relation to the whole, can provide us with new patterns. The visual meshing of the layered and dynamic pattern provides fresh extensions and developments. Thus we see that the nature of process is order. Order is in our internal model, and the external manifestations of this order (i.e. drawings) test the feasibility of our ideas while simultaneously creating new stimuli to be ordered.

One of the most fundamental kinds of order seen is symmetry. Symmetry, at first apparently over-ordered, i.e. stable, is nonetheless a useful element in a vocabulary of transformation as we play with reflection, echo, rotation, repetition, concentricity, etc. Concerned as it is with balance, it is perhaps the first conceptual device we employ to order experience. And so we apply considerably more attention to an asymmetrical problem in an unconscious search for symmetry and balance.

Our ordering leads us to build up a picture of the external world. At the same time the ordering is a projection of the dynamic ordering of our internal model. Thus our ordering of the polygonal grids, with its complexity of levels, implying both lines and planes and with a dynamic interpretation of all parts, may provide us with an external model of the internal system.

From past experience of regular polygonal nets (square and hexagon) we are able to predict the character and substructure of similar patterns (octagon, etc.). We have established an open-ended ordering process and have experimental knowledge of the behaviour of specific types of nets. Faced with a new stimulus, we are in a state of receptivity and 'imbalance' — a dynamic state of 'flow'.

The addition of identical units to each face of the pentagon in accordance with previous processes results in some unexpected behaviour (patterns of one, two, two, one as previously described on page 18). Not only this, but the concentric expanding pentagons show alternating inversion of the nucleus. These two formations with their properties of repetition and symmetry have begun to regularize our initial state of perceptual confusion, and our internal system, utilizing dynamic direction, is moving towards balance. We are also aware of the emergence of the diamond negative shape projecting from each point of the nucleus. As it starts from a point in the nucleus and is a symmetrical shape we can predict that it will end on a point of a further nucleus. The pattern represented by the one, two, two can now be extended to one, two, two, one. It is a more direct link between the end of the repeat and the beginning (one = one) so that we have created a new layer, and this shape appears to fluctuate between figure and ground. It begins to act as a positive whole. Our experience of the character of pentagonal nets is now operating on two distinct but related patterns, and a more fundamental order is needed to create a balanced end-state. Our recognition of the developing patterns has been a result of a process of selection, discrimination, elaboration and synthesis of the incoming stimuli that seemed directly relevant to solving the problem.

At a less differentiated level of perception, the whole pattern and its interrelationships combined with its significance to the operator may have already registered on the internal system. This sensory activity of a more generalized and diffuse nature forms a background of connections upon which the more specific processes are heightened and brought to our conscious awareness.

It may only have needed the congruent internal fluctuations associated with the movements of the diamond shape to 'project back', fusing with this nebulous pattern. At the same time we 'see' in our internal model the centre parts of the pentagonal units joined. The substructure has been understood.

This more subjective part of the process, more allied to intuitive and inventive thinking, has provided the links and allowed us to see a more fundamental structure. Its simplified symmetrical and balanced nature, along with useful predictive properties (with regard to other irregular nets, see nonagon) provide the received end-state which our internal system was motivated to acquire.

The visual meshing of the layered and dynamic pattern provides a new but related element (figs. 2, 4, 5) with potential for entirely fresh extensions and developments. The internal system is again in a receptive state.

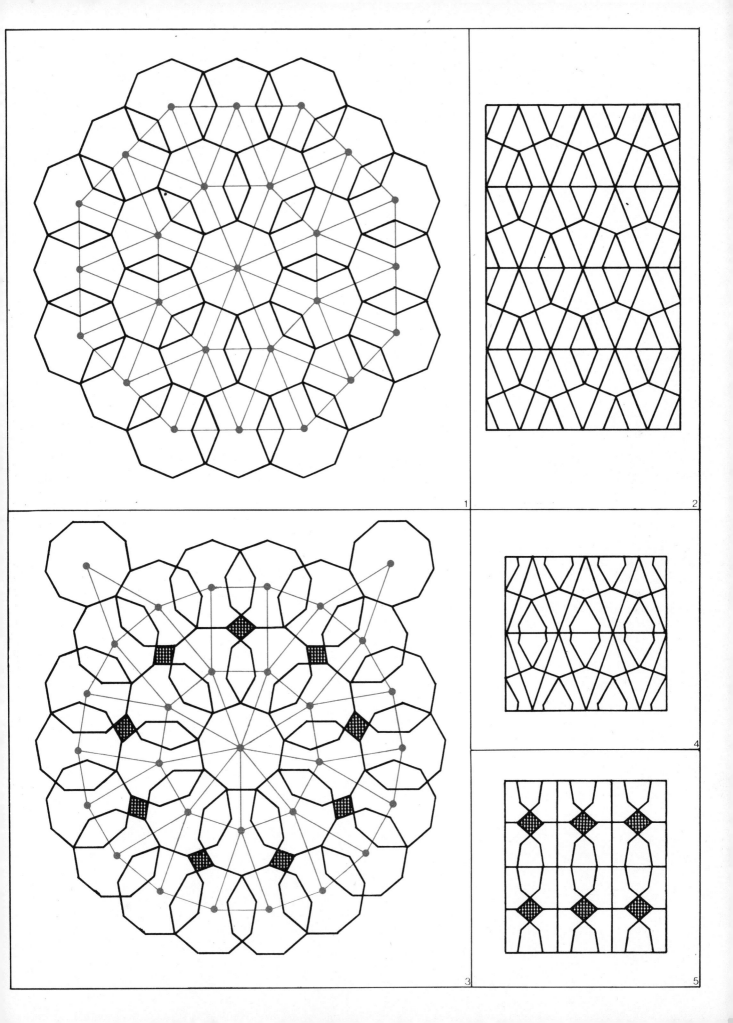

1

2

3

4

5

While exploring the visual patterns associated with numerical relationships (and vice-versa) we have also explored a number of sources, for instance visual patterns in nature translated into numbers and then transformed into graphs, and number progressions or series transformed into graphs and related back to our growing families with numerically or visually similar characteristics.

Opposite we take, as a more complex pattern source, a number series which has fascinated mathematicians and artists since its introduction by Leonardo Fibonacci (Leonardo of Pisa), who brought it to Europe in 1228 after studying mathematics with the Arabs. It begins with, say, one and the previous number (nought), which are added together so that the sum (one) forms the third number. Then the process is repeated: this number (one) is added to the previous number (also one) producing the next number (two). Then two and one form the next number (three), and so on. In full numbers this produces a rapidly ascending graph (after only twenty numbers the number is 4,181). By employing cabbalistic reduction, however, we can hold the graph's upswing and see the rhythm exposed.

The top line in fig. 1 opposite is the reduced Fibonacci series relating to the first irregular graph (fig. 2). Although there is a repeat symmetry of twenty-four units the graph has a very irregular form, of little use in our context of pattern-making. However, if we divide the first series into halves, and then make two series using alternate numbers, a pattern will emerge. This process is repeated with the second part of the original series. Fig. 1 shows the two resultant series, and figs. 3 and 4 the relevant graphs. The two strands of the series reveal separate characteristics, accounting for the apparent irregularity of the whole. The first group has perfect mirror symmetry, while the second (seen in the graph) has inverted mirror symmetry on either side of the figure nine. In the first series we see that the sum of numbers in like positions in each half is nine. Similarly, in the second series the sum of numbers in reflecting positions is also nine. These simple graphs are generated with the two co-ordinates at right-angles to each other. However if we take the number series and apply it to square-grid graph paper in an anti-clockwise direction (i.e. counting vertically for the first number, then horizontally for the second, down for the third, across for the fourth, up for the fifth, etc.) we generate a 'spiral' graph pattern. Figs. 5, 6, and 7 illustrate the whole series and the halves so transformed. The same process is employed on hexagonal graph paper generated by the same number series (figs. 8, 9, 10). Immediately we see a relationship emerging between number series and pattern.

Before we take this any further, we should point out one other major feature of the reduced full number series. We see in fig. 1 two runs of numbers beginning eight, eight, boxed in blue. This series was initiated by nought plus one plus one — one is the reflection number of eight, i.e., one plus eight equals nine. If we examine the boxed series we see that a series beginning with one will generate within itself a series beginning with eight, and vice versa. Prior to one at the start of the series is nought; prior to eight is nine; prior to one later in the series is nine. Thus as we have implied earlier, there is a close relationship between nought and nine (cf. fig. 6, page 9).

0112358437189 88764156281 9112358437189 88764156281 9

125478 874521 0 13831 9 86168

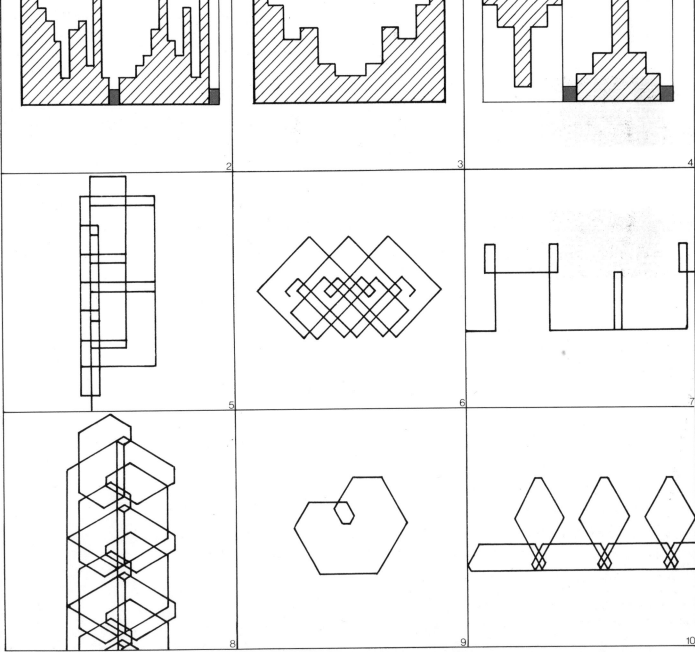

The question that immediately arises is whether, if these events occur in a one, or reflection eight, series, they also occur in series beginning with other pairs of numbers?

On the facing page we see that they do, but that the patterns so generated are unique to the numbers beginning the series. Here we see the characteristics of two and seven describing related patterns (by the fundamental structure or process of the series).

0224617865279 77538213472 9224617865279 77538213472

241857 758142   0 26762 9 73237

There is, however, a very noticeable change in character when the three, six, series is explored. It is much simpler in its internal structure, and although all the previous patterns clearly relate and are operating, if we had based our examination of the Fibonacci series on a series beginning with three we would have failed to see many of the more complex patterns. Thus we see that the complex or disordered image is likely to yield more information than the stable or ordered one.

In fact, so simplified is the structure of the three, six, series that it forms a much shorter repeat unit (graph) and a less elaborate motif (spiral graph). It is unique in the series in that it creates closed units of pattern as against linear developments (see figs. 8, 9, 10 opposite). The relationship between three, six, nine is very close indeed, as we have seen in the Vedic square.

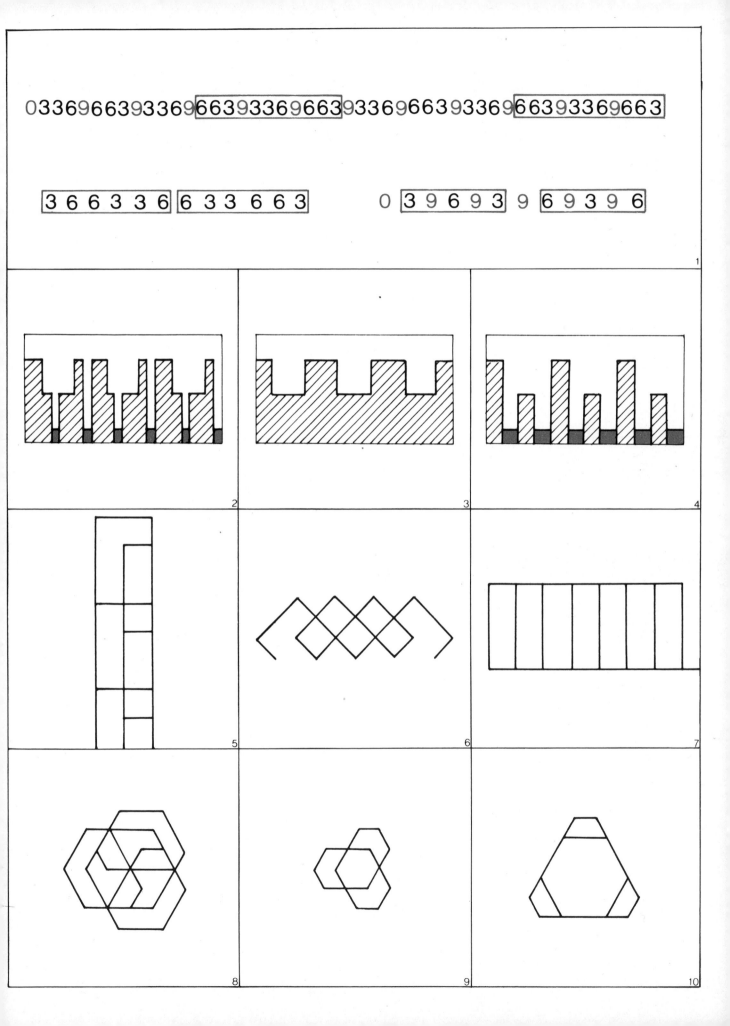

Here the same range of events occurs as in the previous Fibonacci illustrations, but again we have a unique series for the key numbers, four and five. Four and five describe the fulcrum of the reflection system and form the 'fattest' shapes on the Vedic square.

0448325731459 5516742685494483257314 59 55167426854

4 8 2 7 1 5 5 1 7 2 8 4   0 4 3 5 3 4 9 5 6 4 6 5

The complexity of the Fibonacci series prompted new transformations which can now be applied to the pattern within the Vedic square, the starting-point of our enquiry.

Illustrated opposite are graphs derived from the first four lines of the Vedic square. The first is number one to nine repeated. This is then developed spirally on square graph paper and then on hexagonal graph paper. The same process is employed for the second, third, and fourth lines. The patterns formed are of course identical to their pair in reflection; eight, seven, six and five (as in the Vedic square and the Fibonacci series). They are illustrated to demonstrate the characteristic behaviour of each number pair (cf. the relevant Fibonacci number series, especially the third horizontal opposite with page 27). Closer examination will reveal relationships in the rhythms of the 'straight' graphs with those of the Fibonacci series. Examination of the graph will make clear the regular pattern of all the lines even after reduction — note the fourth line: 4, 8, 3, 7, 2, 6, 1, 5, 9.

Although this exploration has perhaps thrown some light on the nature of numbers, there may still appear to be an order within this order which is eluding us. However, in the meantime our vocabulary of visual patterns has been extended, and some thoughts stimulated on the processes that we might exploit to evolve elaborate patterns capable of stimulating concepts of order and unity.

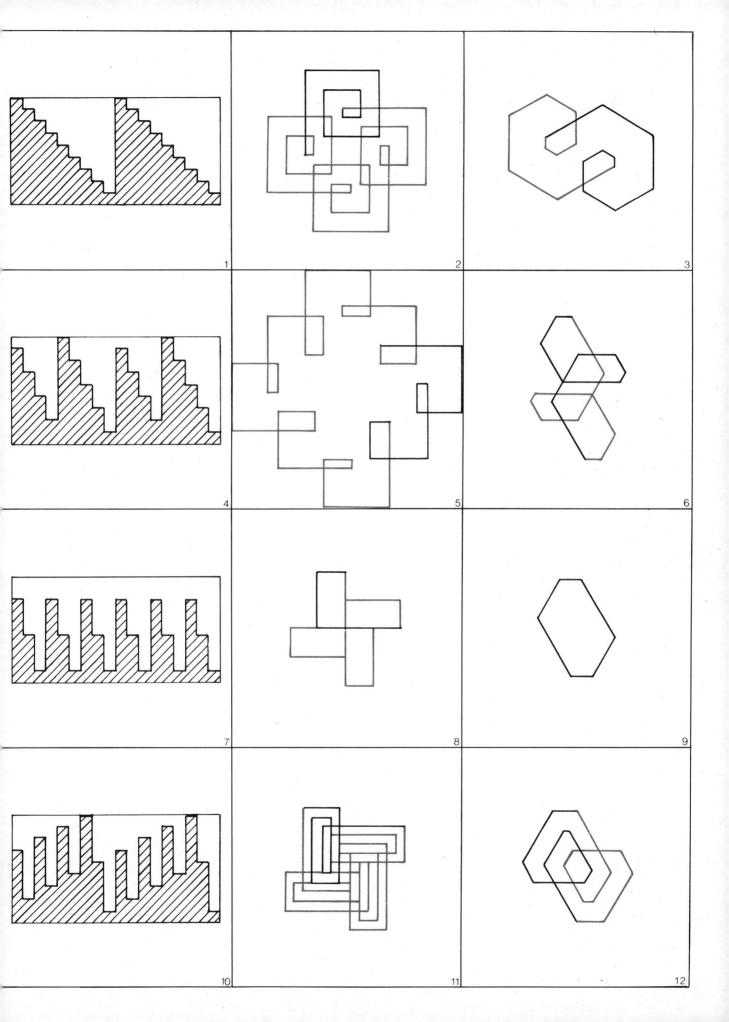

We referred on the previous page to an elusive order within the numerals — a substructure.

Certain peculiarities can be noted in the behaviour patterns of numbers in the Vedic square and the Fibonacci series: the significance of nine; the uniqueness of three and six; the central position of seven, etc. On page 13, fig. 6, we noted that the figures in the diagonals of the square were 1, 4, 9, 7. We saw 1, 4, 9, 7 as the series of square numbers, and 1, 4, 7 as the snowflake pattern (page 17, fig. 8). We also saw that if a series of symbols, nought to nine, continues with one plus nought equalling ten, then nine and nought are perhaps interchangeable (see page 9, fig. 6).

Playing games with the symbols we first multiply like numbers together — one times one, two times two, etc — throughout the series nought to nine; these we reduce (fig. 1 opposite). A clear rhythm of symbols with a central reflection is produced.

Fig. 2 reminds us of the nought and nine relationship and substitutes nought for nine in the series just produced.

Fig. 3 gives us the resulting double reduction and matched numbers nought to nine with the new series (in blue).

Fig. 4 is the Vedic square — a cabbalistic reduction of a multiplication square (see page 11).

Fig. 5 substitutes the new series on the Vedic Square.

At this point the substructure becomes very clear. The patterns of numbers illustrate the form of the square and the character of the pairs of numbers comprising the square. If one then reads off the first, second, third and fourth lines (fig. 6) one finds four distinct patterns taking the behaviour of one, two, three and four. This, if it is a real substructure, should be apparent in any series. The Fibonacci series, being complex, may prove a useful test.

Fig. 7 is four lines of numbers: first, the usual form of the Fibonacci series; second, the same series reduced as previously described; third, the previous line reduced in terms of one, four, seven, and zero; fourth, the splitting of that series in the same manner as we previously split the series, i.e., with alternate numbers forming two series (see page 29).

The result is again a clearer insight into the structure of the series and the behaviour of numbers. The first half consists of one, four, seven, seven, four, one, repeating. This is the number one line of the reduced Vedic square (see fig. 6). As if to emphasize its nature and relationships, the other half consists of noughts and ones repeated. One is the key figure on line one in the Vedic square. Therefore it is emphasized that this is the series of one (or eight).

Fig. 8 takes a series beginning with two, three and four. The first half of the first line is identical to the second line of the reduced Vedic square, the second half is comprised of key figure four (representing two — see fig. 3). The threes are noughts — consistent again.

The first half of the last line is identical with the reduced Vedic square fourth line, and reveals the correct key number.

The concept of key numbers allows us to make many new cross-references, and this we leave to the reader's inclination. Space does not permit us to enlarge this game, which in any case is not central to the argument, but is merely a demonstration of one of many possible games of re-ordering which are the by-product of a way of thought — one which for us developed as a result of studying Islamic patterns.

We have now explored some of the simpler elements of the vocabulary of pattern used in Islamic decoration, such as polygon nets, and in the next chapter we shall look at the vocabulary in use, making up a visual language capable of expressing specific concepts.

0	x	0	=	0	=	0
1	x	1	=	1	=	1
2	x	2	=	4	=	4
3	x	3	=	9	=	9
4	x	4	=	16	=	7
5	x	5	=	25	=	7
6	x	6	=	36	=	9
7	x	7	=	49	=	4
8	x	8	=	64	=	1
9	x	9	=	81	=	9

$_1$

if 9 = 0

0	= 0
1	= 1
4	= 4
9	= 0
7	= 7
7	= 7
9	= 0
4	= 4
1	= 1
9	= 0

$_2$

0	= 0
1	= 1
2	= 4
3	= 0
4	= 7
5	= 7
6	= 0
7	= 4
8	= 1
9	= 0

$_3$

```
1 2 3 4 5 6 7 8 9
2 4 6 8 1 3 5 7 9
3 6 9 3 6 9 3 6 9
4 8 3 7 2 6 1 5 9
5 1 6 2 7 3 8 4 9
6 3 9 6 3 9 6 3 9
7 5 3 1 8 6 4 2 9
8 7 6 5 4 3 2 1 9
9 9 9 9 9 9 9 9 9
```
$_4$

```
1 4 0 7 7 0 4 1 0
4 7 0 1 1 0 7 4 0
0 0 0 0 0 0 0 0 0
7 1 0 4 4 0 1 7 0
7 1 0 4 4 0 1 7 0
0 0 0 0 0 0 0 0 0
4 7 0 1 1 0 7 4 0
1 4 0 7 7 0 4 1 0
0 0 0 0 0 0 0 0 0
```
$_5$

1	=	147741
2	=	471174
3	=	0
4	=	714417

$_6$

0 1 1 2 3 5 8 13 21 34 55 89 144 233 377 610 987 1597 2584 4181 etc.

0 1 1 2 3 5 8 4 3 7 1 8 9 8 8 7 6 4 1 5 6 2 8 1 9 1 1 2 3 5 8 4 3 7 1 8 9 8 8

0 1 1 4 0 7 1 7 0 4 1 1 0 1 1 4 0 7 1 7 0 4 1 1 0 1 1 4 0 7 1 7 0 4 1 1 0 1 1

① 1 4 7 7 4 1 1 4 7 7 4 1   1 0 1 0 1 0 1 0 1 0 1 0 ①

$_7$

② 4 7 1 1 7 4 4 7 1 1 7 4   4 0 4 0 4 0 4 0 4 0 4 0 ④

③ 0 0 0 0 0 0 0 0 0 0 0 0   0 0 0 0 0 0 0 0 0 0 0 0 ⓪

④ 7 1 4 4 1 7 7 1 4 4 1 7   7 0 7 0 7 0 7 0 7 0 7 0 ⑦

$_8$

2 Islamic Pattern

Islamic pattern makes a profound impact upon us, seeming to reveal to us across a thousand years an apparently clear and unambiguous vision — perhaps a vision required by us, certainly one we feel to be relevant to ourselves. The vision — the goal of the internal model — is the knowledge of the ultimate order of an ordered universe.

The Muslims drew knowledge from East and West, from Greece, Rome, Persia, Egypt, India, and China ; and the power to turn this knowledge into wisdom from the principle of unity — the oldest common denominator of these cultures. Islam was not a new religion, but a synthesis and purification. This process resulted in a stronger, clearer vision initially defined by a practical, shrewd and subtle man, Mahomed (born AD 570).

Islam's cradle was the small townships amid the scrub and sand of Arabia — an inhospitable environment inhabited by people who for centuries had led a semi-nomadic existence. These lands were the crossroads of East and West, the nexus of the great trade routes, and their inhabitants were not uncultured. They were as great navigators of the desert as they were later to be of the oceans of the world. It comes as no suprise that they held all natural phenomena in great respect and, in particular, noted carefully the structure of star, plant and rock formations. The vastness of the desert — its immensity dwarfing the caravans of man and beast — developed in these people a cosmic sense of scale and distance in relation to topography and the heavens, combined with a minute order and geometry in their observation of natural forms.

On the facing page we show the visual and mathematical forms in nature in relation to those in Islamic decoration.

Figs. 1, 2, and 3 illustrate a detail of a sunflower seed-head, the double spiral geometry of a seed-head, and the use of that geometry in an early Islamic dome.

Fig. 4 is a copy of an Islamic plant-drawing, showing the geometric analysis of the observed forms.

Fig. 5 illustrates a typical Islamic stalactite dome interior in which we see the development of this plane geometry into three dimensions, paralleled in nature by the cubic crystal formations (fig. 7). The configurations of a decagonal star (fig. 6) and inter-laced squares (figs. 8, 9) are frequently used both within a small-scale pattern and as architectural plans for minarets or tomb towers.

The role of written language in conjunction with Islamic patterns requires some examination. The word was the medium of God's message to the previous prophets, Abraham and Jesus, and the last prophet, Mahomed. Arabic was of divine origin; thus the word in Islam has an importance far greater than in other cultures, and in the arts it was the word — the Koran, poetry and not least conversation — which had precedence. Arabic is a language of great flexibility, fluidity and fineness of structure, and its written form reflects these qualities. It is this flexibility that has ensured its successful survival as the only living source language. It is a musical language whose modulation and textual trans-formations reveal themselves even to the untutored ear and eye.

The visual system of Arabic script is such that it expresses itself clearly in an enormous variety of forms (such as Thuluth, fig. 1, and Kufic, fig. 3) It is legible even when reflection (squared Kufic, fig. 5), interlace (Basmala, fig. 2), repeat (Thuluth fig. 1), and overlay (Basmala, fig. 4) are used in horizontal, vertical, circular, or floral motifs; as borders, medallions or intertwined with brick, stucco, faience and illumination.

For the Westerner, conditioned to buildings expressing strength, weight, and structural honesty, to find lettering combined with geometric and floral motifs covering entire façades of build-ings with a positive plethora of pattern and colour is a visual and conceptual shock. He is astonished to read the two-dimensional surface of an architecture which dissolves before his eyes into ideas more substantial than its reality of brick and faience.

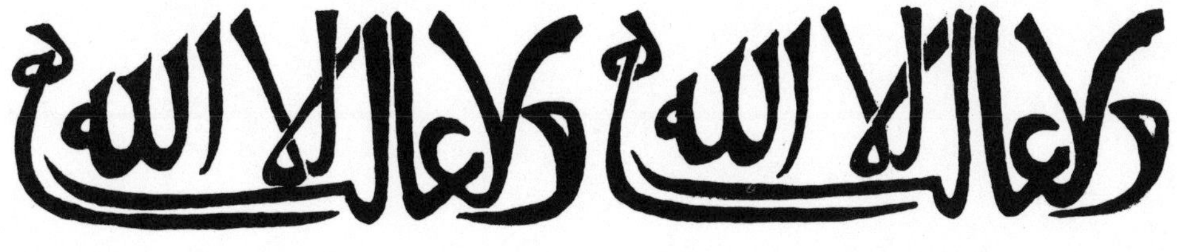

1

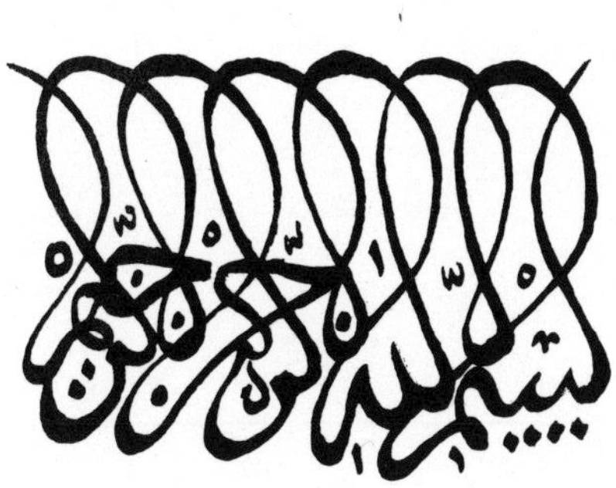

2

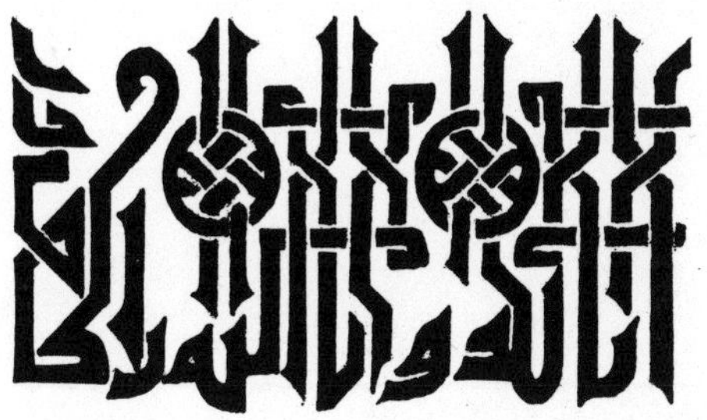

3

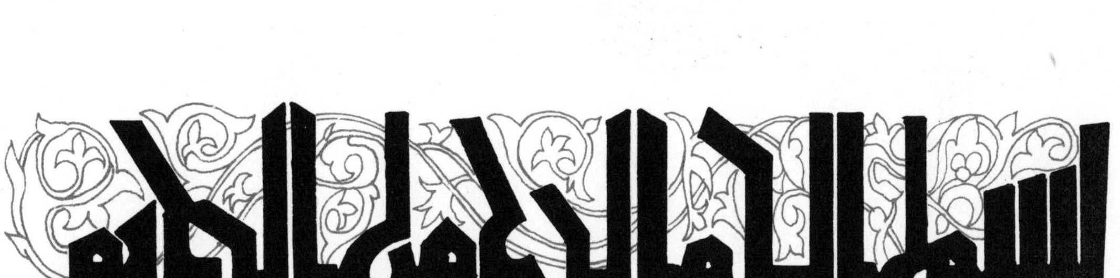

4

5

Early Islamic decoration took many forms and utilized many techniques from the native traditions of carved stone and stucco. But with the brickwork and faience we come to an identifiable language of Islamic decoration, owing little to previous cultures.

The early decoration exploited the brick as a unit, laying it on in vertical, horizontal, angular and circular rhythms; exposing the joint in different widths and at different depths to make the most of the varying densities of shadow. (The illustrations opposite indicate the individual units, and show the basic grids in blue.) This brickwork is unparalleled in its inventive exploitation of a single process. In early monuments the desired complexity and illusionary surface were achieved by a wide variety of simple overall repeat patterns combined with numerous strips of border motif. An extraordinary richness and movement of light and shade was developed by using simple geometric patterns. The minaret patterns from Damghan, Iran (figs. 1–3) illustrate the widening of the interstices of brick to allow stucco detail and finer pattern to be incorporated. During the eleventh century we see the basic vocabulary of grid pattern evolving in brick and stucco, (figs. 4–6, brick patterns from tomb tower at Kharraqan, Iran), later to be developed in faience to a much greater degree of complexity, but with a similar geometry.

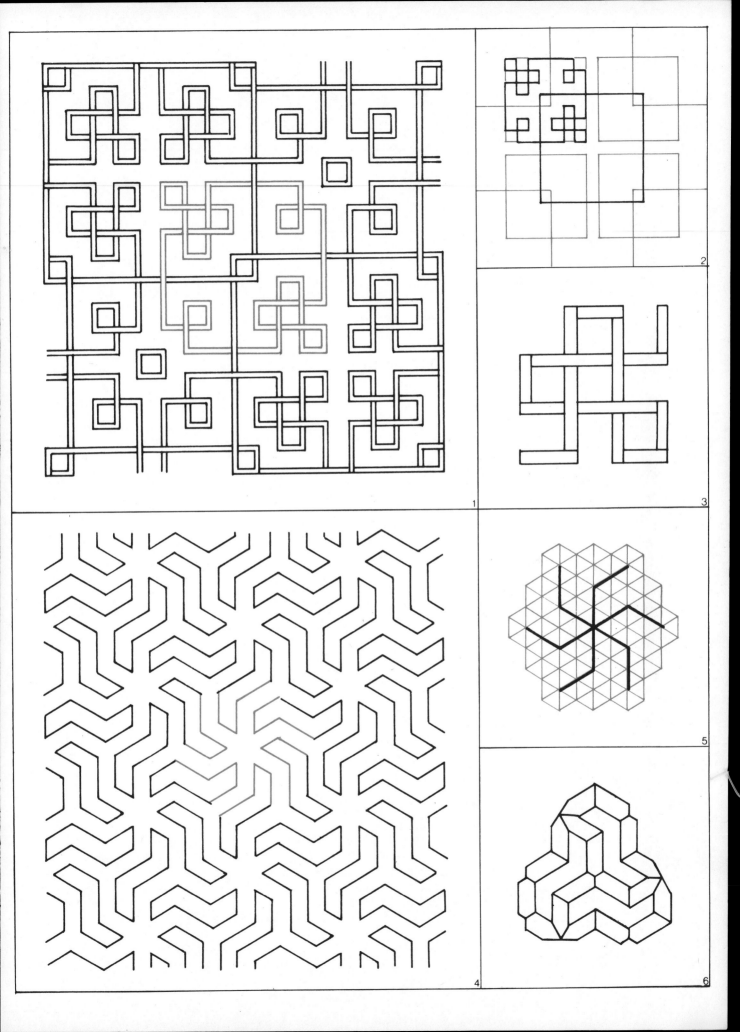

1

2

3

4

5

6

Although brick continued in use over a long period (opposite, brick-patterns and details from the Chihil Dukhteran Mausoleum, Damghan, Iran, figs. 1, 2, and from the minaret, fig. 3), in the fourteenth century we see the incorporation of faience as highlights to the patterns of brickwork, punctuating the monochrome surface with spots of intense colour. Gradually the colour spread and the broken surface was closed by a sheath of mosaic. The illusion of depth within the surface was retained by use of interweaving patterns based upon the brickwork, but now richly coloured. The script appears first as Kufic (brick generated) then floriated Kufic with Nastaliq in stucco (example from Masjid-i Jami, Veramin, Iran, fig. 4), streaming across the façades, integrated not only with geometric pattern (fig. 5, stucco pattern from Masjid-i Jami, Veramin, Iran) but with floral designs, rich material for the designer.

The faience pattern illustrated opposite (fig. 1), from Masjid-i Jum'ah, Yazd, Iran, demonstrates (with analysis in blue) the layered construction based upon a root-two rectangle generating a pentagonal net, which in turn is disguised by the small interlocking elements suggestive of interlace. The resulting pattern (much simplified in these illustrations) has a disciplined mobility.

A similar process is used to generate the interlace pattern taken from a blind window at the Alhambra, Spain (fig. 2), which can also be found in many forms throughout Islam as perforated window-grills and screens. The construction lines in this case are less obvious than might appear (see analysis in blue); the twist of the motif and the manner in which the continuity of the pattern is maintained reveals on analysis two identical grids laid at an angle to each other.

As a ribbon construction this basic element can take many forms, for instance a continual spiralling thread throughout the pattern, or a series of interlinking figures-of-eight.

On the right-hand side of this illustration the reader will note the simplicity of the basic geometry of the pattern: it consists of two spun squares. This simplicity of the basic grid is characteristic of even the most complex patterns.

The window grill or screen is in itself a device to express mobility and transience, as the patterns of light and shade it casts, flow and change continuously with the hours.

1

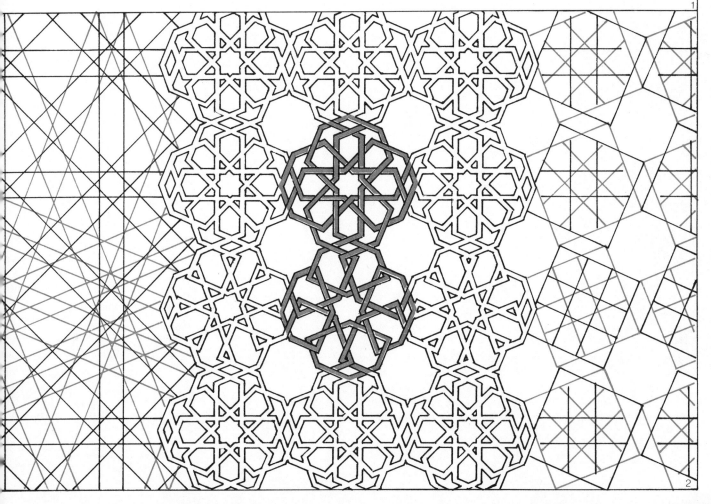

2

The two illustrations opposite are of faience decoration on a mimbar at Yazd, Iran, and show (in blue) the hexagonal net which provides another commonly-used base grid. The top illustration is a fine example of the use of complex interlocking forms, and when looked at for some time reveals patterns within patterns. Although it is basically a flat pattern, an illusion of depth is developed by the apparent placing on top of it of a field of panels of a quite different design. One of these is illustrated in fig. 2, where we see a simple arabesque formed by playing with the compass, and yet appearing to have much more freedom of line than such a construction might imply. The depth in these super-imposed panels of arabesque pattern is achieved by the inter-weaving of two plant forms.

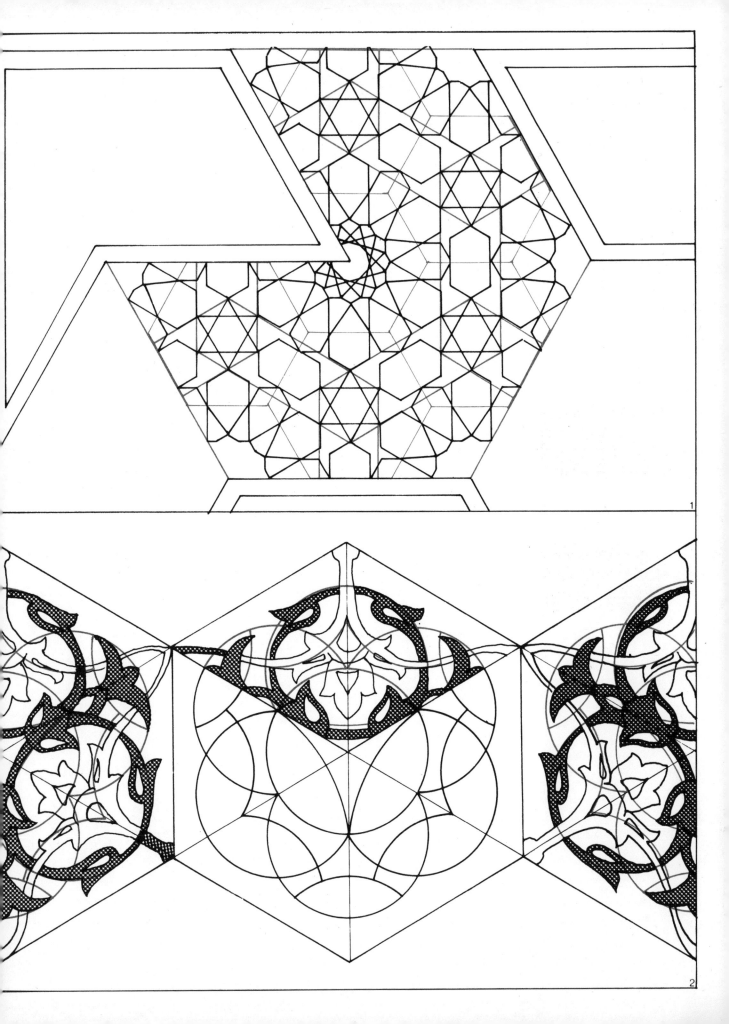

1

2

We can already see in the brickwork and the early faience the use of natural form and illusion to provide increasing mobility — a development leading naturally to the arabesque (opposite, a faience arabesque panel in the Sanctuary of Abd Allah Ansari at Gazur Gah, Iran). The early arabesque faience material has a structure relating to the geometric patterns, and a common base grid. The arabesque and geometric patterns, although used on adjacent surfaces of the building, nevertheless manage to maintain within each panel a sense of their continuity beyond the border of that panel.

The surface of Islamic architecture appears as a continual recession of planes. It is 'theatrical', not in any pejorative sense, but in its use of plane and illusion. These planes and precisely contrived vistas contain subtle volumes. It is as if the surface of the building had many depths.

The arabesque carpets inside the mosques continue the faience themes; but these themes, already elaborate, are in the carpet further intensified because the viewer is closer and can add touch to his impressions. The carpet particularly exploits textures of materials (silk and wool) to incorporate light, producing a shifting sheen of surface and pattern. We are now encompassed by volume described in pattern.

Illustrated opposite are two contrasting traditional carpet designs; fig. 1, a Kashgai carpet from Shiraz, S. Iran, indicates the geometric basis and the parallel with faience; fig. 2, two layers of a medallion carpet from Tabriz, Iran, shows a layered arabesque based also upon a simple grid (in red). The first design (much simplified) is characteristic of the nomadic tradition, which employed within regular motifs complex colour-changes and apparent asymmetries. These asymmetries usually relate to the geometric grid upon which the whole carpet is based. The overall pattern, as with the arabesque, is arbitrarily defined by a border which is unrelated to the main field. This gives the observer the impression of looking through a trapdoor on to a section of the continuing pattern.

The arabesque carpet, particularly those examples produced during the reign of Shah Abbas in the fourteenth century, sometimes developed as many as eight or nine different illusionary layers of pattern.

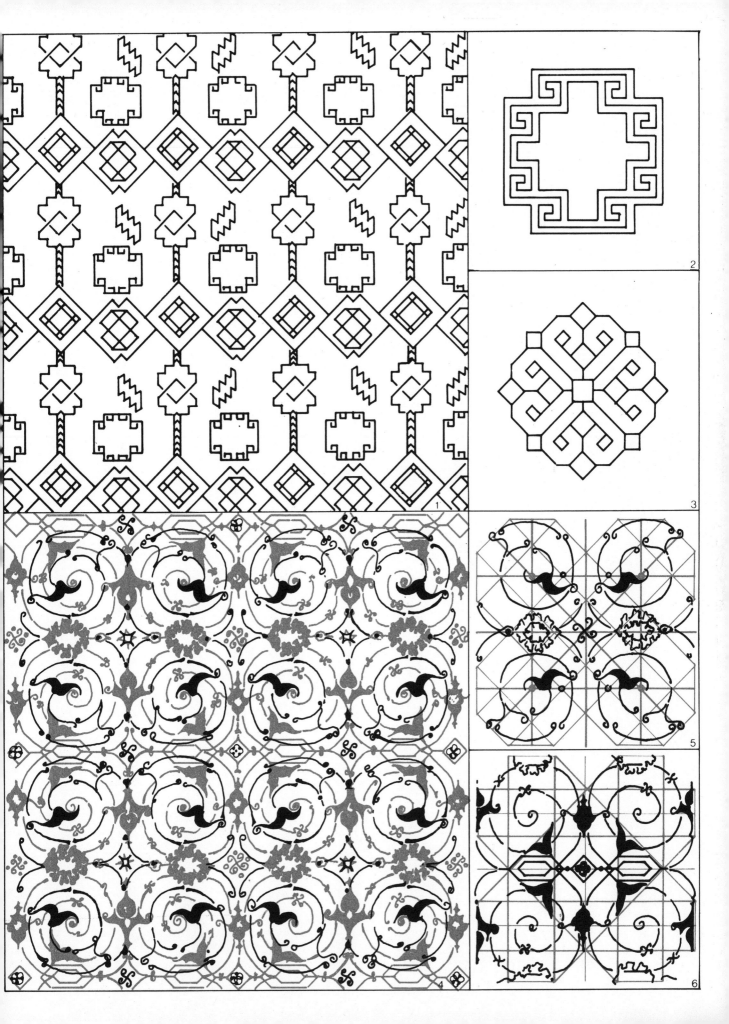

Within, the Islamic building is open-plan and multi-functional; but this openness is only within. The outer world is separated off by high walls and colonnades, protecting the introspective courtyards. The enclosure is a means of increasing the meditative state, and permits the creation of a garden in relation to the architecture — a blend of floral and crystalline patterns.

Illustrated opposite are motifs from a garden-carpet from North-West Iran.

The Koran abounds with visions of Paradise as a garden. An Islamic garden is an artificial paradise, a combination of rational and organic, an expression of the ordered instability we have referred to earlier. It consists of a central axis of water with tributaries at right-angles. A grid of pathways divides the flower-beds and provides a controlled and infinitely varied series of aspects. The flower-beds are sunken so that the plants shall not interfere with the view of the architecture, and also to ensure that only fresh growth is visible. Rows of myrtle bushes provided the water with shade; the fruit trees and vines shade the plants; the evergreen spruces echo the architectural colonnade, and blossom provides both spectacle and perfume.

The intention was to create a living carpet, so that one walked the raised paths with the illusion of treading a path of blossom. Positioned upon this carpet-garden, in carefully chosen relationship to the aspects of the surrounding garden and architecture, were pavilions. They were sited to give the most exquisite views, and were intended to provide privacy for conversation, which was among the most highly-prized accomplishments in Muslim life. The garden embodied many cosmological concepts; it echoed in particular the ancient representation of the world as symmetrically divided into four zones by two axes, forming a cross at the intersection of which is a pool, representing a vision of the universe and a life symbol.

2

3

4

5

Decoration in all media has now become relegated to the minor arts. Yet in Islam we see illuminated script, metalwork, ceramics, textiles and architecture, differing merely in scale, expressing the same vision with a uniform intensity. Whether on a scientific instrument, a carpet, or a mosque, the illusionary layers of pattern, symbol and script allow us to share the vision of the universe which inspired their creation. (For the authors of this book, this vision was communicated through the process of recording the patterns, and only at a later date was their understanding confirmed by written material.) Here was a remarkable visual language speaking across cultures and through time.

The essence of Islamic pattern is not as might at first appear its structure, based upon an ingenious application of geometry; but lies in its use of this abstract structure as an instrument to unify the diversity of experience, encompassing all in one, as a true reflection of Islamic cosmology. The constructions of geometry embody the idea of order without which the greater concept of unity cannot be grasped. The whole is not for most men knowable, but it can be argued that the concept of the whole is essential if we are to order the diversity of experience and deal with the changing realities of existence.

In Islamic decoration there are interrelated layers of pattern congruent with interrelated layers of understanding. These patterns can be seen as models of mind expressing the deeper layers of personality, over and from which experience and memory develop increasingly complex forms. The integrated personality is one which maintains a fluid and creative order, and keeps through this development some awareness of its structure.

The layers of Islamic pattern are drawn extending to infinity, exploiting ambiguity and illusion, apparently dissolving the surface and creating a state of flux within that surface. The designs therefore express the hierarchical layers of existence indicated in Islamic cosmology (see Chapter 4).

In life man can only hope through a continual search to understand and pattern his existence according to the greater design.

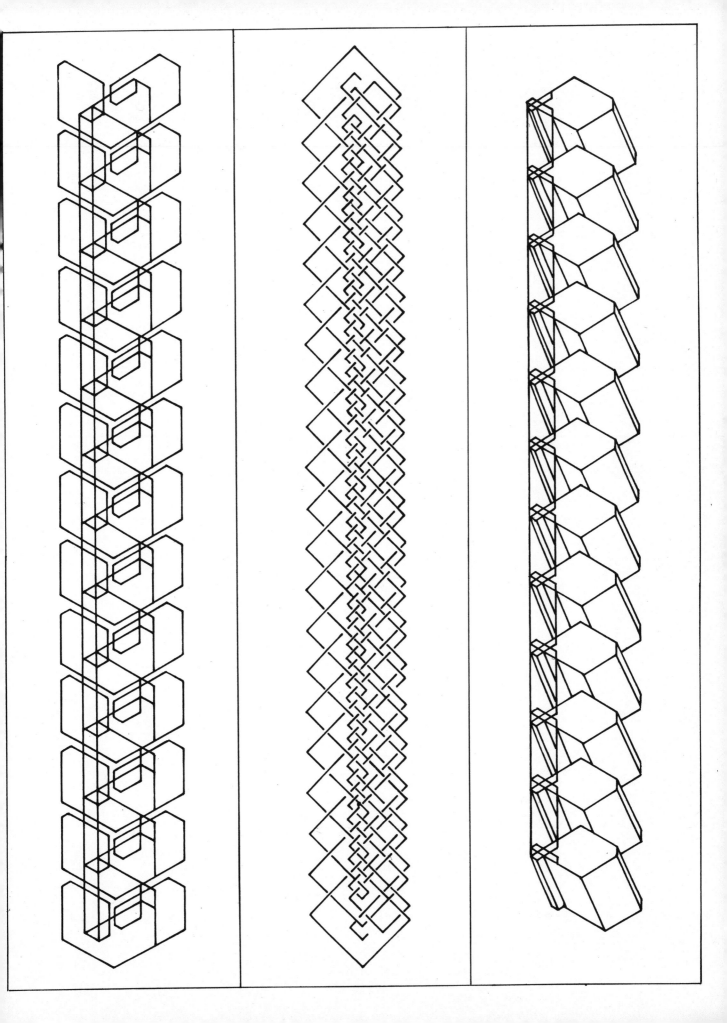

3 Process and Concept

We have so far shown how abstract concepts develop hand in hand with simple processes, and have argued that merely to look at the result of a process (an artifact written or made) is not necessarily sufficient to allow us to gain an understanding of the 'sense of being' of its creators.

Our experience of reworking Islamic pattern gave us a greater insight into the culture of Islam, and at the same time suggested ideas about the nature of thought. In this chapter we shall take the sequential developments begun in Chapter 1 a step further in order to examine the ongoing process, and the role transformation has in its development.

Illustrated opposite are .star-patterns, strikingly common elements in Islamic design (figs. 2–3, an analysis of a dome at Yazd; fig. 1, the final pattern; figs. 4–12, plans and sections of Islamic buildings).

At first glance the dome pattern appears extremely complex, containing in one overall pattern seven-, six-, five-, and four-pointed stars; and yet, as we see in figs. 1–3, the process of construction is simply point joining and selection.

Earlier we explored the Vedic square and the properties of the numbers one to nine. These numbers we applied to the circumference of a circle (see page 13), and then constructed a series of stars by joining the nine fixed points in different sequences, so that the sides of the polygon became chords of the polygon. Each resulting figure had to give direction to one of many routes. If a block was met, reference back took place and the rules were changed. In this way we learnt about the design of games.

With the formula above we produced the nine images illustrated opposite.

Figs. 1 and 8 were formed by linking adjacent points (one-point link); Vedic square line one (clockwise) and line eight (anti-clockwise).

Figs. 2 and 7 were formed by linking alternate points (two-point link); Vedic square line two (clockwise) and line seven (anti-clockwise).

Figs. 3 and 6 were formed by linking every third point (three-point link); Vedic square line three (clockwise) and line six (anti-clockwise).

Figs. 4 and 5 were formed by linking every fourth point (four-point link); Vedic square line four (clockwise) and line five (anti-clockwise).

At this point we had completed the reflecting pairs. The process continued, revealing the relationship between nine and zero in the last figure (fig. 9).

Fig. 9 was formed by linking every ninth point (nine point link) Vedic square line nine (999999999).

These stars have now become a circular graph of the Vedic square (opposite, fig. 10). They are also, incidentally, a nest of Hindu numerical symbols for which the verbal equivalents are: one, Brahma; two, Avyakta; three, Prakrit; four, Makattattra; five, Akasa (aether); six, Voyu (air); seven, Fejas (fire); eight, Jala (water) — a striking example of a hierarchy of geometrical processes paralleled by a philosophical structure.

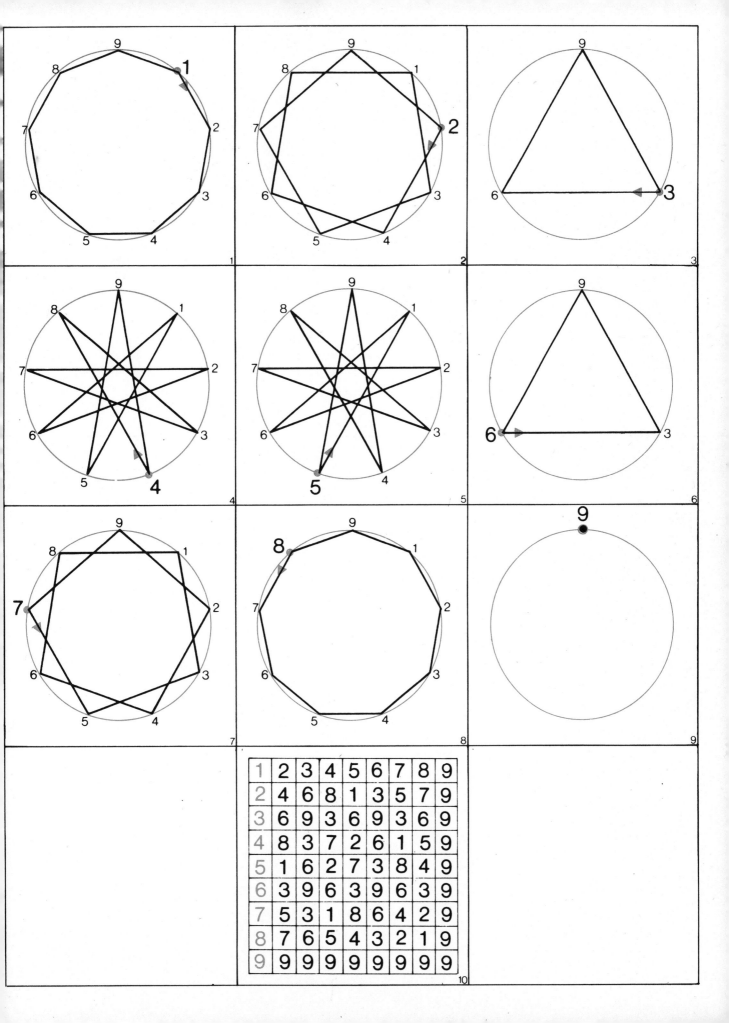

Here we take another process to demonstrate the use of transformation, investigating the relationship of star patterns to their
polygons, three-sided to nine-sided. From any point of a polygon
a continuous line is drawn, touching all points of the polygon
once before returning to the original point. The figures illustrated
opposite were selected for their symmetry.

At the beginning of each polygon's sequence, indicated in red,
are the lengths of lines used to construct the star. From the
triangle (three sides with no possible development), the square
(four sides and one chord), the pentagon, the hexagon, the
heptagon, the octagon to the nonagon, we notice a rapid increase
in the permutations, and many cross-references that enable
families of shapes to be formed. There is also a pattern of movement in the developing stars which interrelates unlike polygons.
From these patterns we understand that the visible generating
process is congruent with the development of a conceptual substructure.

The question is, whether such simple processes as these can still aid our internal model-making, even after we have been bombarded for so long by such a plethora of sophisticated information stimuli, and have become so reliant on our increasingly complex and numerous extensors. That is, can these or similar processes still reveal orders that will allow us to make better use of our proliferating technological aids?

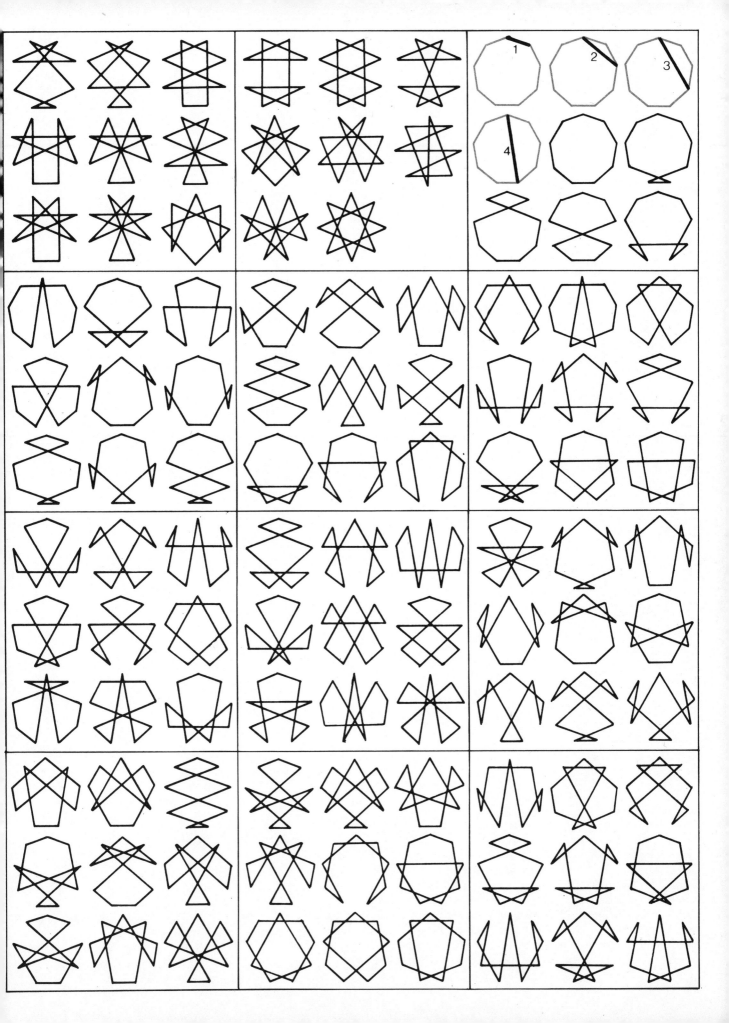

These or similar methods have already proved to be rewarding in creating an ongoing process, an ordered instability within the internal model. One characteristic of superficial levels of ordering is the isolation of the 'subject' derived from an analytical approach. Analysis tends to create an illusion of objectivity and also to prevent cross-referencing of superficially unrelated concepts. It requires a concentrated approach, a focusing of the energies on a predetermined area. While we are not denying the necessity of either analysis or concentration, we believe that creative thought requires the complement of these qualities in the form of synthetic thinking and widening of the area of attention. In our culture more emphasis is placed on analysis, which is understandable because it represents a more obvious type of ordering, and is, besides, identified with the quantifying methods of science. The arts, the 'other half', are qualitative and have been polarized to the extent of apparent disorder. In attempts to close the gap the arts imitate the sciences, failing perhaps to recognize the true nature of their contribution. Beneath the cultural duality of arts and sciences (a very recent phenomenon) there is an aesthetic of being from which they both draw strength. This aesthetic is a fusion of intellect and intuition, analysis and synthesis, a fundamental, dynamic order present in the physiology of the brain.

Perhaps we are now witnessing a change of emphasis, as science deals increasingly with the intangibility of 'reality'. Recent research into the structure of brain rhythms suggests that it is in a state of relaxation of thought that new relationships can be seen, indicating that we should perhaps look more seriously towards Eastern techniques of yoga and meditation, and supporting our questioning of our analytical and quantifying approach.

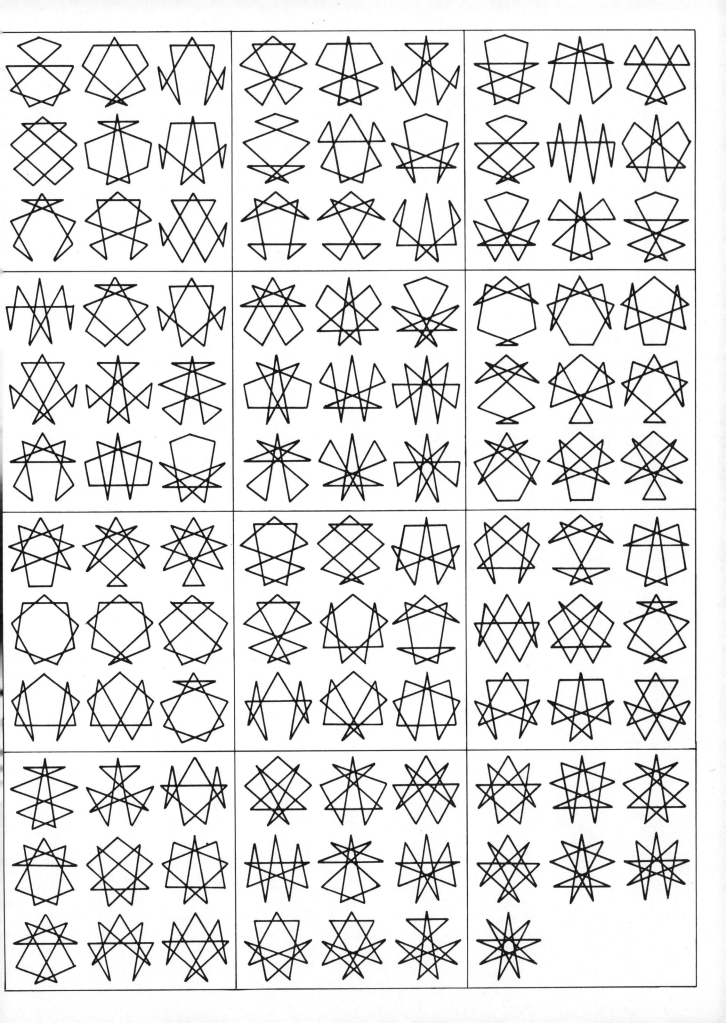

On the page opposite we are using numbers to pattern the stars of the previous pages. The numbers relate to the chord numbers of the stars, and indicate how many of each length each figure contains. (We start to use numbers because the proliferating star systems and their emerging families become so complex that a more compact representation is required.) As the numbers accumulate on the page a visual pattern emerges. This pattern of numerals develops independently of its source, the stars, and then the stars are ordered by reference to the numerical pattern. This process shows the pattern of development of the stars more clearly.

Numbers, as we have seen, are a model of the internal model's organization, externalized as numerals. Our knowledge of mathematics as a self-generating system can now be used in developing other systems.

In the Western tradition of teaching mathematics the units of a sequence are seen as being disparate. What this examination of pattern demonstrates is that it is possible to view each unit primarily as part of a whole development.

Why is it that our internal ordering system finds it so difficult to order continuous movement? Our physical senses are bombarded by stimuli continuously, but it seems we need to stop movement in order to understand it. We 'see' reality like a film still, or at best

a series of stills. Indeed one of our fundamental ordering techniques, numeration, freezes in step-by-step operations much of our concept-building. The arbitrary and divisive nature of whole numbers is a serious handicap to flow-thinking. Those who believe that the discipline of mathematics may one day make it possible to communicate with the inhabitants of other planets (American scientists are at present engaged in constructing a mathematical language for this purpose) should bear in mind the possibility of the existence of beings whose thinking and ordering processes are a continuum, who would view ours as primitive or incomprehensible, bearing little relationship to real experience. We learn at an early age in life to fragment our documentation of experience without questioning the nature of the system. Yet paradoxically, it is through numerals that we are able to inter-relate disparate objects and build the concept of holism. We can, as we have seen, build concepts of layered hierarchies of development interpenetrated by common points (see page 19 fig. 1), and create flow by way of numerals in the graph, and similar processes; but graph and layers, even when combined in two dimensions, are plainly inadequate as a model of reality. We have yet to transform these processes into three dimensions, and by implication, discuss these three dimensions as a cross-section of a fourth dimension.

	Number of chords	Number of figures
TRIANGLE	1	1
SQUARE	2	2
PENTAGON	2	4
HEXAGON	3	11
HEPTAGON	3	24
OCTAGON	4	67
NONAGON	4	192

TRIANGLE	SQUARE	PENTAGON	HEXAGON
111	1111	11111	111111
	1122	11122	111122
		11222	111133
		22222	111223
			111333
			112222
			112222
			112233
			122223
			122333
			222233

HEPTAGON

1111111	1122233
1111122	1122333
1111133	1122333
1111223	1123333
1111233	1133333
1111333	1222233
1112222	1223333
1112233	2222222
1112233	2222233
1122222	2223333
1122223	2233333
1122233	3333333

OCTAGON

11111111	11222233
11111122	11222233
11111133	11222244
11111144	11222244
11111223	11222244
11111333	11223344
11111333	11223344
11111344	11223344
11112222	11223344
11112222	11223344
11112233	11333333
11112233	11333344
11112244	12222223
11112244	12222223
11112244	12222333
11112244	12222333
11113333	12222333
11113333	12233333
11113344	12233344
11122223	12233344
11122223	12234444
11122333	12234444
11122333	13333344
11122333	13334444
11122333	22223333
11122333	22223333
11122333	22223344
11122344	22223344
11122344	22333344
11133333	22333344
11133333	22333344
11133344	22334444
11133344	33333333
11134444	

NONAGON

111111111	111124444	112222244	112334444	222233344
111111122	111133333	112222244	112334444	222233344
111111133	111133333	112222333	113333334	222233344
111111144	111133334	112222333	113333344	222233344
111111223	111133344	112222334	113333344	222233444
111111244	111133344	112222344	113333444	222233444
111111333	111133444	112222344	113334444	222234444
111111334	111133444	112222444	113334444	222333333
111111444	111133444	112222444	113334444	222333344
111112222	111134444	112223333	113334444	222334444
111112222	111144444	112223333	113344444	222334444
111112233	111144444	112223333	113344444	222334444
111112233	111222222	112223344	113444444	222444444
111112244	111222233	112223344	114444444	223333334
111112244	111222233	112223344	122222233	223333334
111112244	111222233	112223344	122223333	223333344
111113333	111222244	112223344	122223344	223333344
111113344	111222244	112224444	122223344	223333344
111113344	111222244	112224444	122224444	223333444
111113344	111223333	112224444	122333333	223333444
111122223	111223344	112233333	122333344	223334444
111122224	111223344	112233334	122334444	223334444
111122233	111223344	112233344	122444444	223344444
111122233	111223344	112233344	133333344	223344444
111122244	111223344	112233344	133333344	223344444
111122244	111224444	112233344	133334444	224444444
111122333	111224444	112233444	222222222	233333344
111122333	111333333	112233444	222222233	233334444
111122333	111333344	112233444	222222244	233444444
111122333	111333344	112233444	222222333	333333344
111122334	111333344	112233444	222222344	333334444
111122334	111334444	112234444	222223333	333334444
111122344	111334444	112234444	222223344	333344444
111122344	112222222	112244444	222223344	333444444
111122444	112222224	112244444	222224444	334444444
111122444	112222233	112244444	222224444	444444444
111122444	112222233	112333333	222233333	
111123333	112222233	112333333	222233333	
111123344	112222244	112333344	222233334	

In Islamic pattern we saw a way of interrelating two-dimensional layers which did not rely on superimposition, but engaged the layers as interwoven lattices with multiple levels. Here, using this simple transformation, we systematically join the points of the polygon to produce stars with a ribbon development which we call roping.

The star system generates a vocabulary of linear patterns, which, though discrete, become closely interrelated through the ongoing process. Once a quantity of these patterns has been generated on the page there is feedback like an exposed length of movie film; each 'frame' gives a glimpse of a process in motion. Though it is not a smooth transition, it gives us a sense of development between adjacent images which allows us to imagine a continuum. The sense of movement is partly due to the sheer number of images on the page — they form an eye-drawing strip cartoon.

The lines of the figures are interwoven so that not only movement but space is implied. The illustrations opposite accentuate this illusion by giving width to the lines and interlacing them. The diagrams resulting from such a simple transformation radically alter the nature of the feedback. The images are now revealed with connections in implied space.

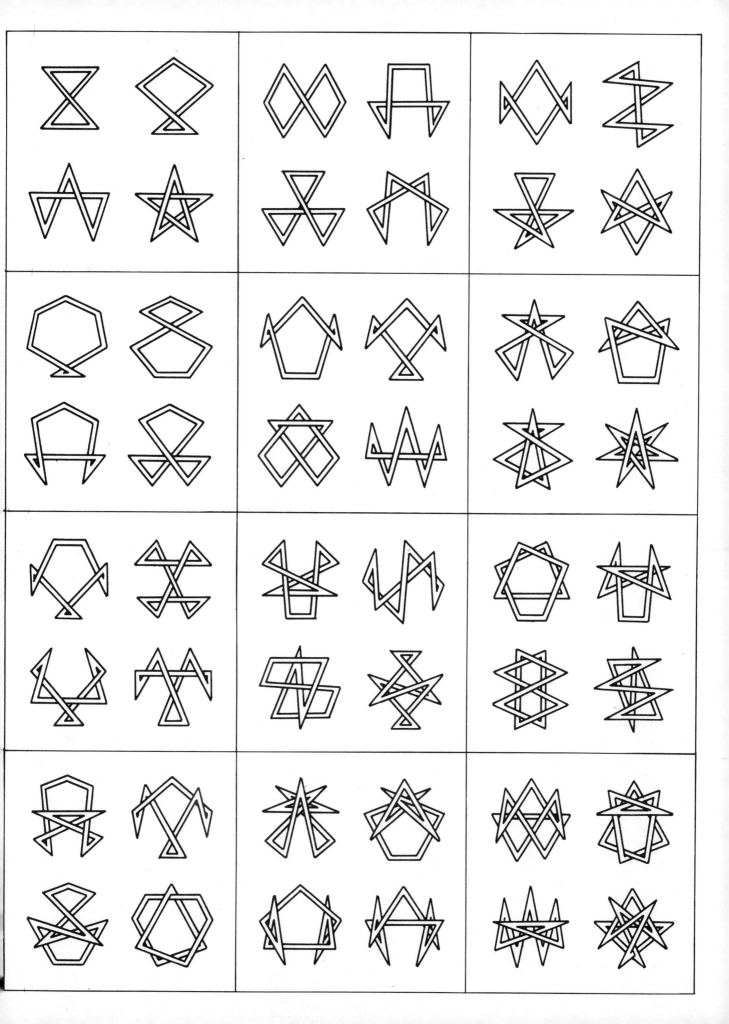

We have seen in the star system in two dimensions the possibility, not merely of cross-relating different polygons, but of seeing them as 'stills' from a process of development from the triangle through to the most complex polygon, and, finally, as an implied ribbon development in space. We shall now return to their use in relationship to each other as elements forming a net or grid.

The illustrations opposite take the simple grids of the hexagon and octagon, and demonstrate the use of the hexagonal and octagonal star patterns to give hexagonal and octagonal 'tiles'. To approach from a different angle, we can take a hexagonal or octagonal net and imprint the individual units with any one of the relevant star patterns, then observe how varied the resulting overall patterns become.

It is striking how similar these patterns are to Islamic decoration, even though the process from which they originate is different. Here we are concerned with developing a vocabulary, while for the Islamic artist the vocabulary was already available and was used consciously to express philosophical conceptions. The basic similarity is in the way of thinking, which can be characterized as an open-ended exploration, a blend of intellect and intuition.

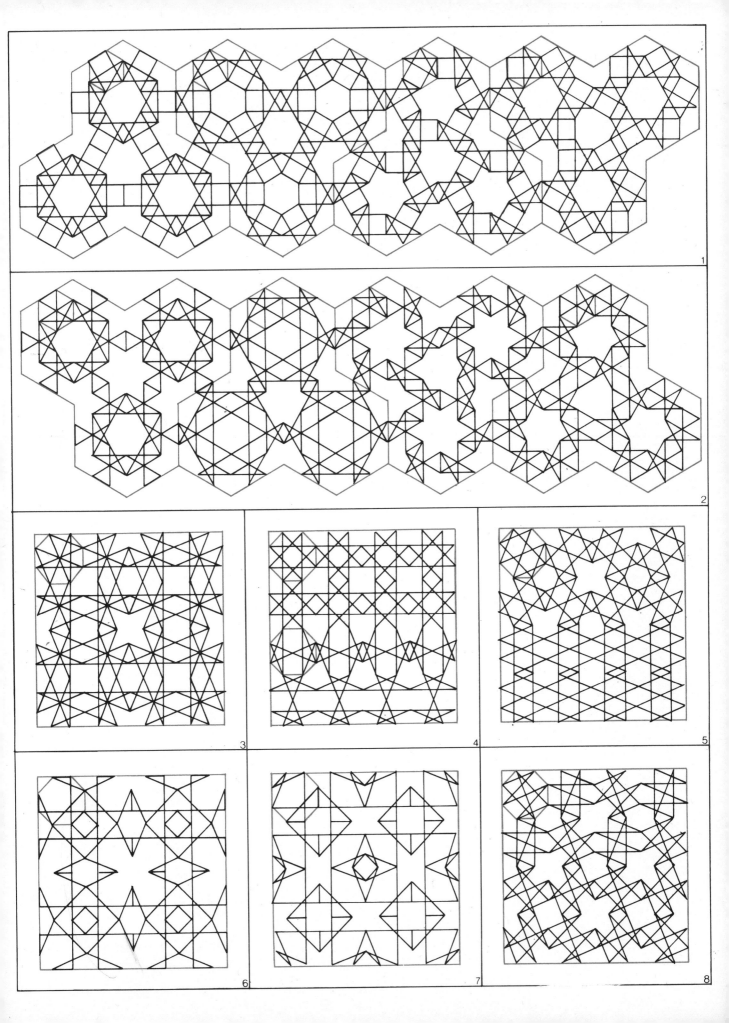

1

2

3

4

5

6

7

8

The appearance of Islamic patterns from a different process sent us back to look again at our earlier processes, in this instance the polygonal constructions. We have seen how every step of the process of externalizing a concept can, at a later stage, be used as a new spring-board for ideas. The first step in the process of drawing a polygon is the use of the compass to draw a circle, the circumference of which is divided according to the polygon required. The first polygonal construction learnt on acquiring compasses is the hexagon. The radius used to inscribe the circumference is also used to mark off in sequence the divisions of that circumference to construct the hexagon. Playing with this process, we developed petal patterns formed by inscribing circles from these points on the circumference.

We next exploited the construction lines only, the arcs from the now theoretical hexagon. After developing the hexagonal stars we have not only the sides of the hexagon but also the chords of the hexagon to act as radii for our circle, and so a rather different series of patterns emerges. Once established as a system, this process is applied to the various star formations. The figures opposite illustrate the results.

The immediate feedback from these drawings is a sense of movement, created not only by the interweave but also in this case by the curved line. These traces, echoing the movement of the compass, describe complex, apparently discrete, multi-layered events, whose movements we imagine as continuous. But these movements, although interweaving, are essentially in one plane. This is due to the circle, which is accepted as such, and therefore seen 'straight-on'. Our previous knowledge of drawing, coinage, etc., prevents us from 'seeing' these circles as ellipses, although we *actually* see few circles. (We tend to read complex ellipses as circles seen from an angle.)

The circle is therefore not so ambiguous as we might expect, compared with the square. There is a strength in its process/concept which has made it a positive key to concepts in the shorthand of symbols. The circle is perfect symmetry in two dimensions.

We have seen how our concepts really began to develop after our internal model had received sufficient data to stimulate us to externalize them, as by notations, etc. These external manifestations reveal self-generative systems for tackling extended versions of the original problem, without need of new external data. This produces an amplified, self-generating system in our internal model which affects both the external model and the incoming data — i.e., it modifies our view of reality. So all three elements of thought are involved in complex transformations. The pivotal transformation is that in the external model.

We have already seen above that dimensional changes can provide a means of conceptual transformation — from zero dimension (the point) to the first dimension (the line) and the second dimension (the plane). Our next step is into three dimensions. It is frequently assumed that since we live in a three-dimensional world we can see 3D; but according to our earlier observations we should only be able to see a cross-section, i.e., two dimensions. It is evident that in fact we assemble views of objects by moving our viewing position, or, failing this, rely on prior knowledge to build a hypothetical model of the object. This leads us to many curious misunderstandings of the world of objects.

Our binocular vision, though it aids our model-building, can also mislead us — witness the apparent increase in the width of a cylinder of x diameter when it is held beside a flat card of x width. This effect is caused by our eyes, being set apart, looking slightly round the cylinder on both sides. A sculptor tends, in his early training, to pay too much attention to the silhouette, and fails to consider the cross-section. In fact the external model commonly used to supply our ideas of three dimensions is an assembly of two-dimensional cross-sections — usually parallel slices through the object (as in contour maps or models), or intersecting planes at right angles (as in mock-ups of new designs for vehicles, etc.). It is no coincidence that, in the second case, the right-angle is used, as it emphasizes the projection of the idea from two to three dimensions.

Even the two-dimensional surface of an object can only be understood in terms of cross-section of the object it defines. However, to say categorically that we only 'see' two-dimensionally is not wholly accurate, for binocular vision and movement are important in extending our abilities. Added to this we have already noted how the two-dimensional world is capable of deformation implying three dimensions.

We can postulate that a painting is in fact $2\frac{1}{2}$D — the half representing the illusion caused by colour advancing and receding, and illusions of figure-ground reversal and depth.

Man analyses and synthesizes the elements of surface and cross-section to comprehend the object. Immediately we think of 3D we tend to bring in touch stimuli. In building our model we are aware of our physical movements (or hypothetical physical movements) around the object and tend to 'feel' our way to understanding it. Sight and touch are indeed closely related; vision, it seems, is in evolution a sophisticated development of the touch sense.

Perception of the external world and our experience of its three dimensions is not merely a question of one, two, and three dimensions but also a matter of scale. As a means of transformation scale is closely allied to movement. We have developed lenses etc. to explore without physical movement a wide spectrum of size phenomena, each level being a transformation of another. Even without extra lenses, vision and prior knowledge create layers of experience related to scale. We shall see how touch gives way to sight.

First we have the hand-held object whose form can be determined quite accurately without sight by multiple touches; second, we have the object too large to be handled easily, requiring multiple views and changes in the angle of vision; third, we move round the large object (for example, a small building) assembling from many movements an internal model which we have never 'seen'; fourth, we move within parts of an 'object' (say a city) which is too big to allow us to retain accurate sensory information about its totality. Finally, there are objects which are too big to see such as the Earth, requiring that the internal model be based on information other than the directly visual or tactile. In the last instance, now that we have developed the necessary extensor to take us away from the Earth our previous internal model may require considerable modification. Similarly with our ideas of the 'micro' end of the scale.

Man sees himself as in a midway position in the universe. Micro is part of him, as he is part of macro. The centering of himself, and the ease with which this concept is held in two extremes may have something to do with his concepts being scaleless. Thus we find affinity between the views of atomic particles and cosmos.

Movement, i.e. change in the physical or mental position of the viewer to give changes of scale, can be a powerful agent of conceptual transformation.

The illustrations opposite represent another movement towards the concept of 'mind' within the external process of drawing.

We have now returned to the polygonal nets and their relationship with and transformation into polyhedra.

Simple polygons can form the faces of a solid if we fold up a net of polygons. Here we take a truncated tetrahedron which has four major faces (hexagons) — one hidden from view — and four minor faces (triangles). On each major face we draw the hexagon construction lines (see fig. 1). This pattern is the simplest interlace of rings. These interlacing patterns are larger than the face, extending beyond the original hexagon. Thus the construction lines of each face intersect those of the adjacent face. To make this construction clearer we show both the dynamic traces of the construction lines and the equivalent silhouette (fig. 3).

The second group of drawings (figs. 4–6) shows the use of a hexagonal star development, transformed into interlaces and applied as above.

We have now created an implied cross-section of a bubble-structure relating polyhedra to curvilinear form, and flat to curved surfaces. Thus the circle begins to operate within our transformation system, giving by its axial symmetry its three-dimensional spherical form to the evolving structure. Each of these curved lines or planes intersects others with a substructure of straight line and plane.

The model begins to indicate the time element when it is seen as a glimpse of an ongoing process, and allows further developments of our parallel idea-game. No longer is it necessary to divide point from line from plane, or straight from curved, or large from small; all interrelate in the continuum of the internal/external model.

At this point, the polyhedron still appears a discrete model, but its base geometry can be transformed to give any of the space-filling solids with the flanges of the arcing intersecting adjacent polyhedra, altering the inner structure of those polyhedra and of itself. It can therefore be seen as an equivalent in three dimensions of the two-dimensional nets described in the first chapter.

1

2

3

4

5

6

4 Islamic Constructions

Now that we have arrived in three dimensions it is appropriate to look at some examples of Islamic architecture and see how they can be related to the early cosmology.

We see in the diagram opposite (fig. 1) a stalactite formation from the Mosque of Süleyman I, Istanbul, showing how from a simple hexagonal grid successive projections of elements have given a complex three-dimensional structure which acts as a zone of transition between the earthly cube and the heavenly sphere of the dome. This symbolic representation did not originate in Islam; it was developed from Eastern and Western sources, including Byzantine and Hindu, and in this it is representative of the synthetic character of Islamic culture.

The stalactite formation is peculiar to Islam, and it was developed in many permutations. The plaster and timber stalactite half-dome (fig. 2) from Ali Qapu, Isfahan, is formed by a similar process of projection from two dimensions. The dome is developed as a light form made up of micro-domes, which are here perforated by bottle-shaped recesses intended to improve the acoustics of a music room.

This architectural model is paralleled in the cosmology expressed in the writings of the tenth-century Persian experimental philosopher, Ibn Sina. Ibn Sina's vision of the universe was of a cosmos of symbols through which the seeker for divine knowledge must travel. The cosmos was not seen as external fact, but as an interior reality. Islamic cosmology was of 'being' compounded of intellect, soul and body. There was not the separation of Creator and created which continually divided the Christian tradition. From unity of being can come only Unity. To describe apparent differences a system of 'layering' of development was evolved. These layers, however, were merely devices to make developments

comprehensible, not horizontal divisions (cf. the interlace of patterns).

Al Biruni, a Persian contemporary of Ibn Sina, lived for some years in India as court astronomer to Mahmud, and wrote some one hundred and eighty works covering mathematics, astronomy, optics, medicine, mineralogy and pharmacology. No single method was sufficient in his restless search; he studied the scriptures and the ancients; he observed, experimented, analyzed and reflected. His was not simply a search for knowledge, but an attempt to evolve, through knowledge, closeness to God. The open-ended goals of this process were the knowledge of the nature of God and the conception of unity in the cosmos.

Al-Biruni saw nature as a force which formed and ordered matter within a pattern of unity. Everything had its contribution to make; there was no waste. This order could be perceived by many routes; a fundamental one was the innate counting ability by which difference became evident. He was not, however, a Pythagorean who gave mystic significance to numbers; but from observation he noted the frequent appearance of certain numbers and series in different contexts and, from this observation, gave significance to those numbers.

Concepts contained within his numerology included the hierarchy of solids: one, the cube, six-sided (square) and earthy; two, the icosahedron, twenty-sided (triangles) and watery; three, the octahedron, eight-sided (triangles) and airy; four, the tetrahedron, four-sided (triangles) and fiery; five, the dodecahedron, twelve-sided, and containing all. But his numerology and his interest in astrology were the result of acceptance of a hypothetical problem of ordering the unseen orders, rather than articles of faith or dogma.

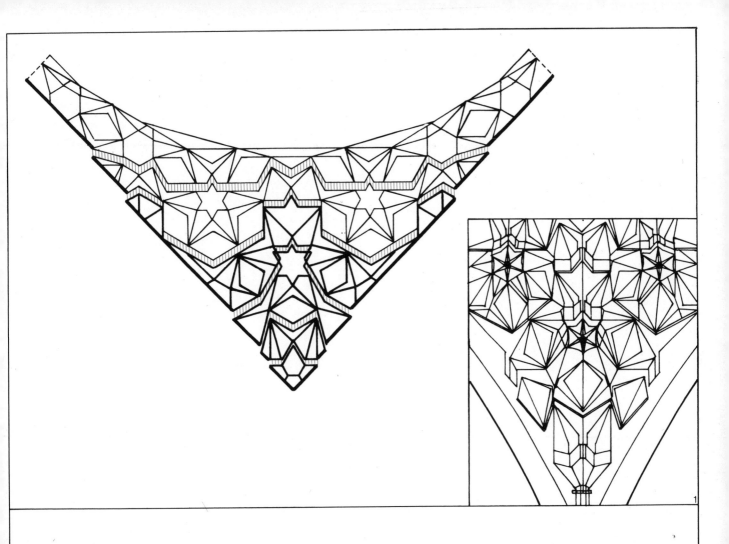

1

2

Ibn Sina described 'orders' of the intellect as each one leading to a lower order, the whole infused with the emanation of being and ordered by nature as governing agent and integral part. He described how the first point, when acted upon by nature, extended to form a line, which in turn was acted upon to form a plane, and thence to 'body' (in our terms, 3D). However, he did not stop here but, seeing nature as movement and soul as order, implied the next layer of 'body' in movement (analogous to what we call the fourth dimension).

Illustrated opposite are the analyses (figs. 1 and 2) and drawing (fig. 3) of the interior of a dome in the library vaults of the Hasjid-i Jami, Isfahan, Iran, and (figs. 4–6) of a dome at Bursa, Turkey. Here the star pattern is used as the basis for an entire dome in which the micro-structure of the stalactites (their two-dimensional plan shown in red) dissolves the possible finality of a severer form. Here we see again the dome, the external model, used to suggest the concept of hierarchical layers and to increase the progressive interiorization of the viewer. The structure, physically finite, encourages through its implications of unity and infinity a meditative state in which the viewer can feel himself part of the whole, and conceive of infinity as a continuum.

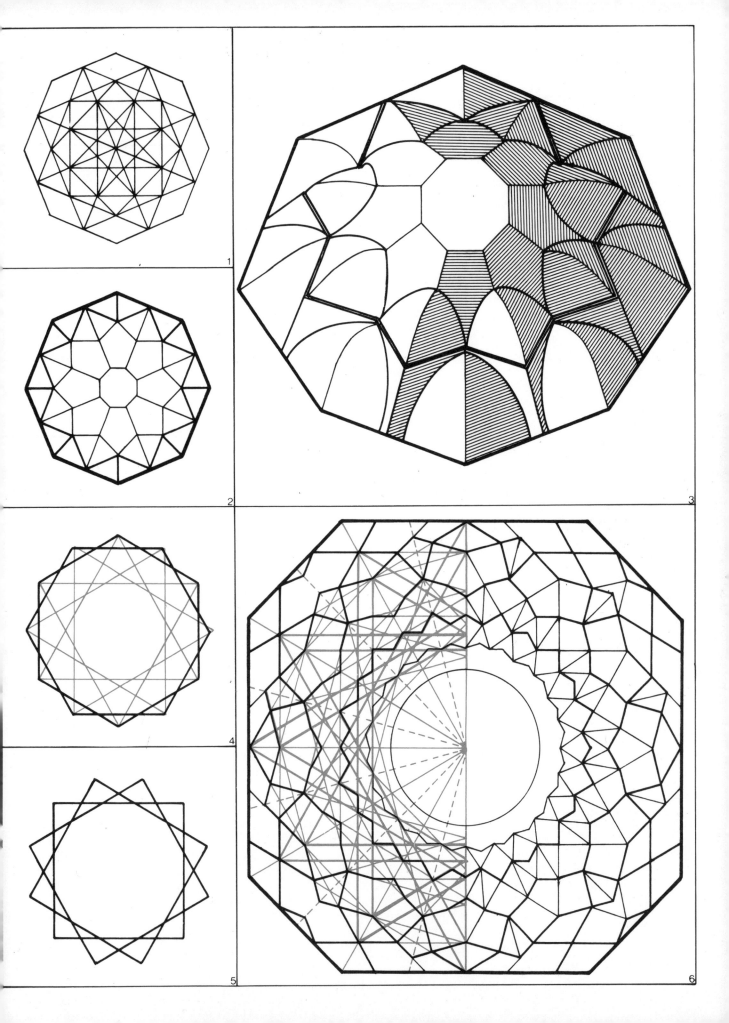

1

2

3

4

5

6

The characteristics of nature Ibn Sina described as the hot and moist, and the cold and dry. He constructed a model of concentric spherical development away from the amalgam (the source, the whole, the centre), and noted the gradual lessening of the hot and moist (as the movement became less) and the increasing of the cold and dry. He saw natural forms as echoing this model. The essence, thinly disposed in stones and crystals (being cold and dry and therefore subtantially inanimate) developed intensity towards the organic (which is hot and moist, and therefore animate, i.e. generating life) the nearer to the original source it becomes. The Earth he saw as having fallen through successive levels, away from the source, and having cooled down in the process until the mineral solids coalesced at the lower level.

Unfortunately when we read astrological symbols or see early diagrams of the humours we may fail to reach the underlying deduction, which at that time could only be expressed in such terms. When Ibn Sina uses the circle or square it is a key to his vision of the cosmos; the circle expresses a continuum of movement and is therefore the most perfect of forms; the square is rigid, earthbound and therefore cold, but could nevertheless return up through the layers of development back to the circle, via the pentagon and expanding polygons (see page 91).

The organic and inorganic form implied in the hierarchy of humours is expressed on the outer surface of the Islamic domes.

This is illustrated in fig. 1 opposite, the arabesque dome at the Masjid-i Shah, Isfahan, Iran, and fig. 4, the dome at the Shrine of Shah Nematullah Vali, at Mahan, Iran, with their analyses (figs. 2 and 3).

For modern man it is tempting to disentangle the medieval concept of the 'humours' from apparently more scientific studies; however, for these experimental philosophers, this separation would have appeared absurd within the concept of unity. Their philosophical search for truth was the motivation for their systematic research into the nature of matter. The arguments surrounding the nature of matter ranged from the theories of the Atomists to those of the Geometric schools. For Ibn Sina the argument was resolved by accepting potential divisibility (necessary for understanding) while recognizing the actual impossibility of division. Similarly time is not divisible. There are no discrete atoms of time. Time is a measure of motion. Motion implies matter, the absence of which implies space; but here again, while recognizing the potential existence of space, Ibn Sina also recognized that in practice space does not exist. Nevertheless, it is potentially measurable. He refers to nature's abhorrence of space in connection with the impossibility of creating a perfect vacuum, and in the persistence with which nature attempts to fill any contrived vacuum. This *horror vacui* is echoed in the Islamic custom of covering with pattern all empty surfaces.

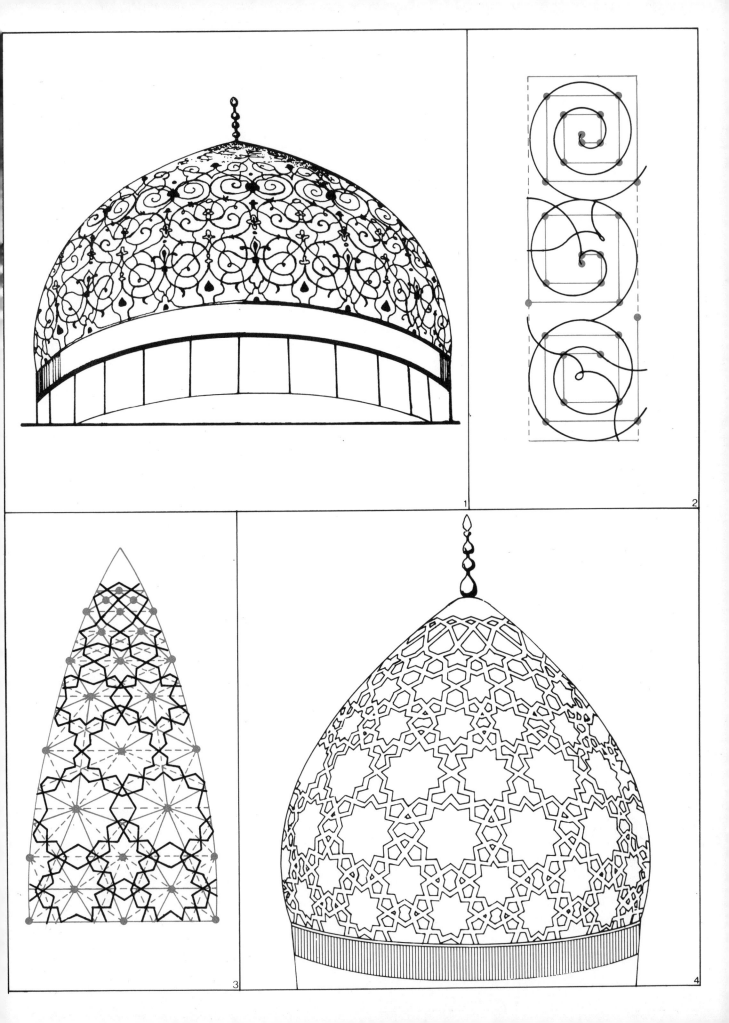

1

2

3

4

Although Islamic architecture appears to place great emphasis upon surface, its surfaces describe volumes. As the surfaces are given depth through the use of pattern in two dimensions, so the resulting volumes are given a further dimension by the use of illusion. Fig. 1 (the Gunbad-i Alt at Abarqah, Iran) is a solid sculptural mass which is lightened by the subtle recession of planes, false windows and implied perforations. Fig. 2 (the Masjid-i Jami, Isfahan, Iran) illustrates the 'theatrical' nature of the architecture, showing the recession of planes and the use of stalactite formations to further dissolve the potential weight of the building. The surface is decorated with coloured faience.

So we can trace in these patterns processes which offer to the mind's eye a structural yet infinitely variable development. All phenomena are related through different levels, as matter moves or is moved towards perfection (the source; the whole). When inanimate nature ceases to be thought of as having life (as in Renaissance schools), when a distinction is made between inanimate and living, then the gnostic view is destroyed. When the 'governor' of being (nature) fails temporarily to order and balance, then what we call evil occurs. The true sciences have therefore to relate the outward manifestations to the inner aspect, with the relationship of each particle to the universe. Experimental philosophy makes use of observation, experiment, and reason, in trying to understand the manifestations of cosmological principles derived from 'intellectual intuition'. Man is a microcosm of the cosmological principle — not merely matter with life added.

1

2

Fig. 2 (a column cap from the Alhambra, Spain) is a high-relief carving describing the order seen in plant forms; fig. 3 (also a column cap from the Alhambra) is the transitional stalactite form describing a geometric development, and fig. 4. (a column cap from Yazd, Iran) is an emblematic device combining both those elements, and reminiscent of the faience patterns.

With his understanding of the experienced world of illusion the Muslim travels towards the true reality, until the heat and light of the source transform him. Physical disorder, for him, can now no longer occur; and because his soul, in its ordering capacity, illuminates areas of knowledge of past and future events, his wisdom becomes a part of the Whole.

Such ideas owed much to the Hindu concept of the unfolding of time, each thing manifesting itself at the cosmic moment of its unfolding. The Muslims developed this hypothesis to include a cyclical notion of time, with each phase producing its creation; the creation generated by the sun, ordering chaos not only in days but in great cycles of historical and geological change (each race, for instance, appeared at a different cycle of time). The 'feeling' of these ideas is expressed in the arches of the Umayyad Mosque, Cordoba, Spain (fig. 1 opposite).

1

2

3

4

Islamic cosmology was a synthesis of the available knowledge of both East and West, accessible to the Muslim through the astonishing advance of his Empire in the century-and-a-half from AD 630, when it spread rapidly from Arabia to Spain on one hand and from the Middle East to Northern India on the other. The Muslims held in their great libraries the major works of all previous Mediterranean cultures, as well as the Hindu, and eventually the Chinese. A synthesis was made possible by a respect for all knowledge, encouraged by the Koranic injunction to contemplate heaven and earth, which God had created by Truth, and by a flexibility of thought encouraged by the Koran's insistence upon the transitory nature of the world.

As the Muslim travelled, absorbing the new experiences of alien cultures, he erected buildings which, though recognizably Islamic, employing in particular the visual language of decoration, nevertheless integrated the native forms and traditions (see illustration opposite, Humayun's Tomb, Delhi, India). The use of water is a reminder not only of the source of all living things, but an emphasis on transience, when the building is seen in reflection.

The Muslim travels between the East (pure form) and the West (earth), until he can see the essence of things as intelligible, and therefore the outer form of those things as symbols of being.

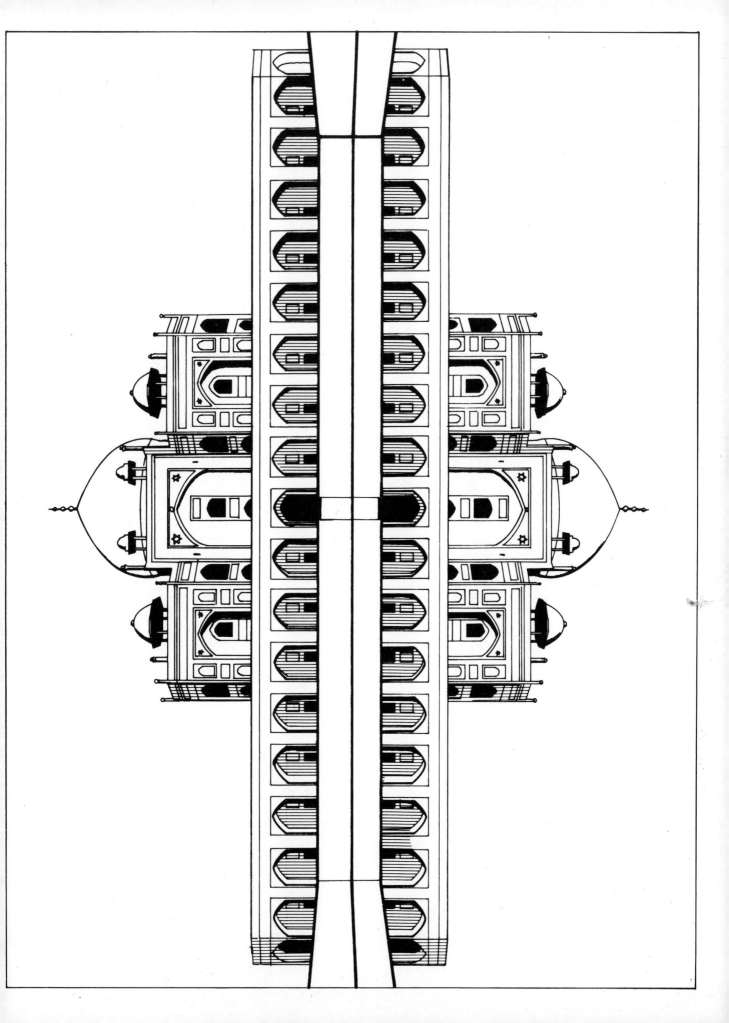

5 Structural Developments

In this chapter we continue the development of three-dimensional patterns begun in Chapter 3.

The superimposition of the first seven polygons (i.e. from three-sided up to nine-sided) illustrated opposite allows us to see the close relationship of these discrete forms as a development. Here we can read various interrelating movements. The polygons are generated by circles, each with a radius larger than the preceding one, to maintain a consistent side length. The development can be interpreted, and ordered, as a diagram (see opposite) which then encourages prediction of further developments. The top half of the diagram shows the construction of the polygons. The semi-circles are divided by the number of sides of the desired polygon. From the centres of the semi-circles lines are drawn to intersect these divisions on the circumferences. The rectangles and triangles in red are seen in the sub-nets of each polygon as demon-strated in Chapter 1. We can view this diagram as a simple expression of an expanding situation.

In understanding expanding situations, then, the size at any particular stage is not important, but the nature of the expansion is; hence the development and use of ratios, angles, deformation, symmetries and dimensionless numbers in modern mathematics. Numeration of the parts of a system will tend to fragment it and increase, rather than decrease, disorder.

In any situation, a social system for example, we must see the *whole* as the primary layer and endeavour to relate the parts to the whole before comparing one part with another. In designing systems one is concerned with the dynamic arrangement of parts rather than with how to add part to part. Nature, and not magni-tude, should be our emphasis in dealing with problems, if we are not to tie our solution to one part only.

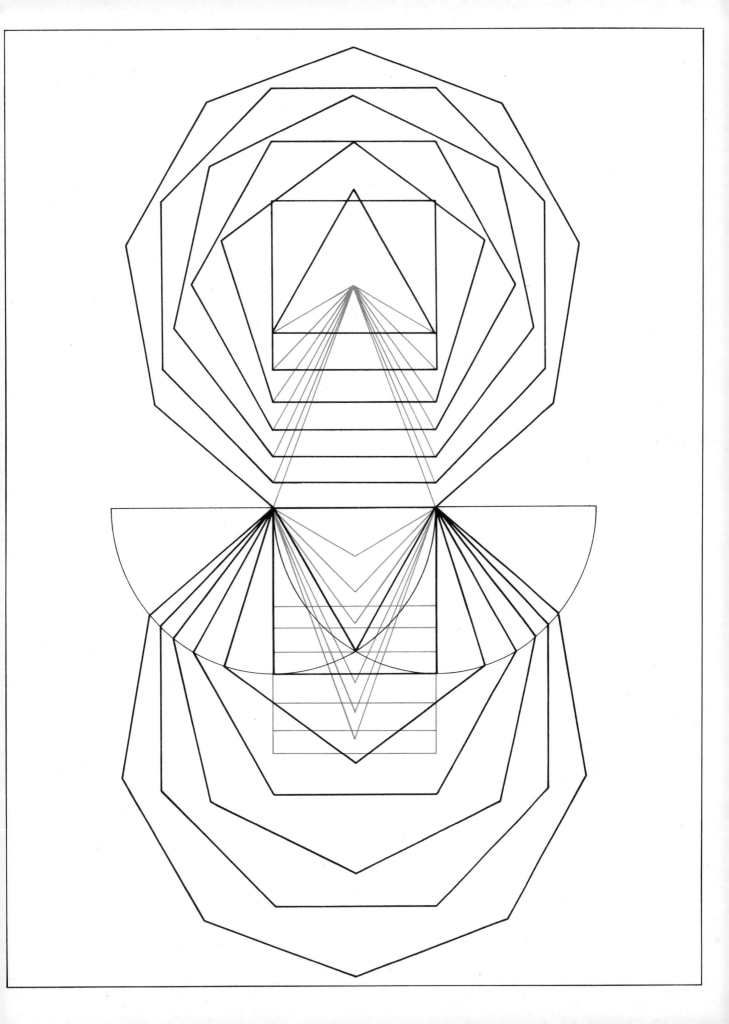

We see in the illustration opposite a table, across the diagonal of which are the familiar star patterns of the developing polygons of constant side length.

If we consider the concept of a circle drawn on a surface then we know it, in one of its aspects, as an angle having 360 degrees; this is a flat circle. What, we may ask, is a 'circle' of more or less than 360 degrees? A circle of less than 360 degrees can be seen, after we have removed a segment of n degrees from our paper circle and rejoined its circumference, as making a cone. So we can now talk of circles as part of a development from a vertical 'rod' (one dimension) as a nought degrees circle, through cones in three dimensions, to our flat paper circle in two dimensions of 360 degrees. We now have, via our external process, a means of increasing the 360 degrees circle. That is, we now insert a segment of n degrees, so transforming the 360-degrees circle into the 360-degrees-plus-n-degrees circle. This creates a bent or warped surface which becomes increasingly complex in its curvature with each segment added.

If we now refer again to the illustration, we see to the right of the diagonal the reduced circles (the cones), and to the left the increased circles (the deformed circles). On the cones we have drawn the star patterns and show the height (elevation) of the cones in red (the plan is black). In the top right-hand corner is the plan view of a cone, which originated in the bottom right-hand corner as a nonagonal star, and has had excised from that flat figure six segments of the nonagon, leaving, after rejoining the circumference, a steep conical form. The six phases of this development are shown in the right-hand column. Each column can be read vertically as a star (illustrated on the diagonal of the table) increasing in size below the star and decreasing above the

star to form, on the top horizontal line, a triangular cone; on the next horizontal line, a square based cone, and so on. Thus on the bottom horizontal line all the figures have nine sides, ranging from the nonagonal star (right) to the nine-sided 'triangle' on the left.

Clearly, from such a table very complex forms can be ordered and interrelated, and from this nucleus of a system, prediction can be generated of layered polygonal developments.

Instead of quantifying to describe the system we use angles (see table), so that the conceptual boundaries between square and pentagon begin to dissolve. And with this dissolution we find a new way of generating 3D from 2D through movement. We have deformed the physical page which had generated through illusion the games with stars illustrated earlier. On page 95 the two systems are brought together. The illustrations are enlargements of alternate units from the table, reading both vertically and horizontally. We can see in a small sample the development of forms and their possible relationships to the whole.

The concept of curved space current in our cosmology (Einstein) is frequently illustrated as deformations of plane geometry. It is the basis for much of our higher technology and is now employed extensively in the sciences to understand all phenomena from resonance states within field particles to the emanations of super clusters of galaxies. Nowadays these disciplines have to build conceptual models related to traces, or effects, of the the unseen phenomena. These mathematical models are very different structures from the traditional external models. From these different external models we must develop different internal models, and if we are to re-integrate our knowledge then these models developed by the specialists must be available to the layman as a shared view of the cosmos.

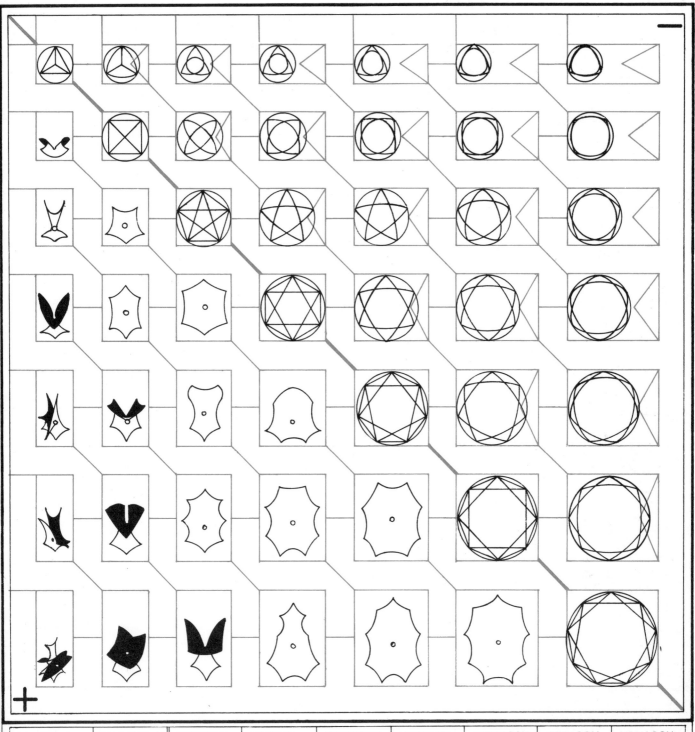

NUMBER OF SIDES	DIAMETER OF CIRCLE	TRIANGLE 120°	SQUARE 90°	PENTAGON 72°	HEXAGON 60°	HEPTAGON 51$\frac{3}{7}$°	OCTAGON 45°	NONAGON 40°
3	4	360°	270°	216°	180°	154$\frac{2}{7}$°	135°	120°
4	5	480°	360°	288°	240°	205$\frac{5}{7}$°	180°	160°
5	6	600°	450°	360°	300°	257$\frac{1}{7}$°	225°	200°
6	7	720°	540°	432°	360°	308$\frac{4}{7}$°	270°	240°
7	8	840°	630°	504°	420°	360°	315°	280°
8	9	960°	720°	576°	480°	411$\frac{3}{7}$°	360°	320°
9	10	1080°	810°	648°	540°	462$\frac{6}{7}$°	405°	360°

LENGTH OF SIDES $\frac{7}{2}$ or 3$\frac{1}{2}$

Metaphorically speaking, we are living in two different worlds — one the continuum, the other a series of cross-sections of that continuum; the former the whole, the latter the part. This discontinuity is aggravated by our tendency merely to quantify, exalting statistics, and by the jealous guarding of academic preserves. From an emotional and a practical point of view we must develop fresh and fluent ordering systems to deal with the continuum of the social structure.

The hardware of society, the external model, will then develop true to the internal model. We must recognize and exploit the qualitative possibilities within the whole system (i.e. the aesthetic of mathematics) and educate ourselves in dealing with the continuum to develop vocabularies of transformation.

These vocabularies can be developed by means of simple processes (and they need to be simple to get behind the now almost self-generating technology we employ as extensors). We have become progressively divorced from building our own external models and use more and more pre-programmed extensors. The structure of these extensors now exceeds in complexity the material they deal with, and we cannot understand the technology which we are using to develop ideas.

Television is an extensor whose virtues and vices are endlessly discussed in relation to the material it processes. The danger of television is in the acceptance of this medium as a substitute for inter-communication. While it pours out a necessarily simplistic view of reality, because of its highly transitory and non-referrable non-modifiable process, it aggravates social isolation. By using it as a simulator of reality we reduce the input of fresh stimuli. Simulation is becoming a twentieth-century substitute for transformation. But we must see simulation as illusion — not confuse the fake with reality but rather use it constructively in a state of 'willing suspension of disbelief' (Coleridge). The question is how best to re-integrate our extensors so that they operate creatively. Television, for example, is best used if accepted as a distorting mirror of events, dramatically increasing our viewing positions and stimulating internal and external model-making.

A major influence on our conceptual process is architecture, the most cumbersome and physically restrictive extensor. We have seen in Chapter 4 how Islamic architecture both embodies and stimulates philosophical concepts. How successful is our own architecture in matching our conceptual development?

If we continue the development of the drawings we can see what they will suggest as architecture. On page 92 we began with cones and warping planes generated by a notion of a circle having more or less than 360 degrees. Fig. 3b opposite shows a polygon (a square) split with two segments inserted before it is rejoined to create the complex curved surface of a polygon of six sides (a 'six-sided square'). Fig. 3a shows an alternative way of inscribing such a form — here the 'thick sides' of the square (three by one unit strips) are used, lapping one-third of each in sequence around the square, and securing it with a stapler. In place of paper the authors used a plastic sheet twelve feet by four feet, and an industrial stapler for fastenings. These light-weight units were then stapled together to form a structure sixty feet square and twenty feet high (fig. 1, drawing of a discotheque-theatre built in the South of France, 1967). Flat panels were clipped into the snouts of the structure, and one had a building.

Figs. 2, 5 and 6 show three examples of polygon clusters with their associated star patterns which, in multiples, can form the desired complex curved forms. The strength of the form is in the spring of the material.

In Chapter 3 we saw the development of stars into interlacing arcs. Fig. 4 is a reminder of the interlace generated by the sides and diagonals of the square. This is, therefore, a transformation of the star patterns and can be treated in the same way as the flat circles. In fig. 7 we see three six-sided 'square arcs' forming a complex three-dimensional form. This is generated by a very simple process, and the form illustrated is the simplest of its level of generation. The implication of these arced forms is that they could be interlacing separate rings. The physical model of this idea holds itself together and can form an open lattice (fig. 4). On arriving at the model (fig. 7), we find that the once-separate rings now form continuous strips interweaving in space. Thus another possible extension is seen. We have seen how the *construction* lines of a simple drawing can be exploited to form decorative patterns which in turn become the physical structure, leaving the original curved plane behind and appearing in space as a single continuous strip. (Incidentally this final structure is simplicity itself compared with a piece of knitting or crochet work. Examination of knitting, with its inherent dimensional changes, will reveal a host of implications which could be exploited on a larger scale or in a different context.)

We have now used the illusionary nature of drawing to suggest a three-dimensional form which, when constructed, is transformed by movement, implying in turn the loss of the surface and the building of the lines upon that surface in space. In the previous chapter (page 83) we saw the $2\frac{1}{2}$D surface star patterns lifted off the flat plane stretched round the dome, implying a rubber geometry (topology). With these continuous curved surfaces we used the cellular concept of the stalactite: a $3\frac{1}{2}$D continuum of form.

In fig. 3 opposite we see the cube (edge on) upon whose faces we have inscribed, on either side of the diagonal, arcs bisecting the edges of the cube. This pattern is drawn so that the curved lines link up on adjacent faces (a half-face unit is illustrated in blue). We now read that drawing of a cube with the line pattern indicating cuts through the cube. The cut cube can now be reassembled (fig. 2). Although the curved lines were intended to indicate a curved solid form within a solid cube, we have built the model in 2D card, a two-dimensional assemblage in three dimensions, as the original drawing was a one-dimensional assemblage in two dimensions. We now unfold the card model (see fig. 1).

Thus complex curved forms can be generated which have their substructure in the cube, or vice versa. They can be constructed within the axial geometry of the cube as convex or concave surfaces, with the other side describing concave or convex flat facets. But we have already implied that in our present cosmology, even this extension and interrelation of curved and flat forms is insufficient if we require multi-axial systems. However, this system extends the concept of the cube and can be deformed according to the deformation symmetry of the cube.

The remaining illustrations show the three major deformations and the resulting family of forms, now extending into multiple axial arrangements in space.

The forms are all interrelated and can be used together via their common 'face' geometry, which, beneath the apparent complexity, is very simple. The first 'family' uses only the half-square illustrated in red — a right-angled isosceles triangle with a quarter-circle cut. The remaining families merely incorporate an equilateral triangle of the same edge size with one-sixth circle bisecting two sides.

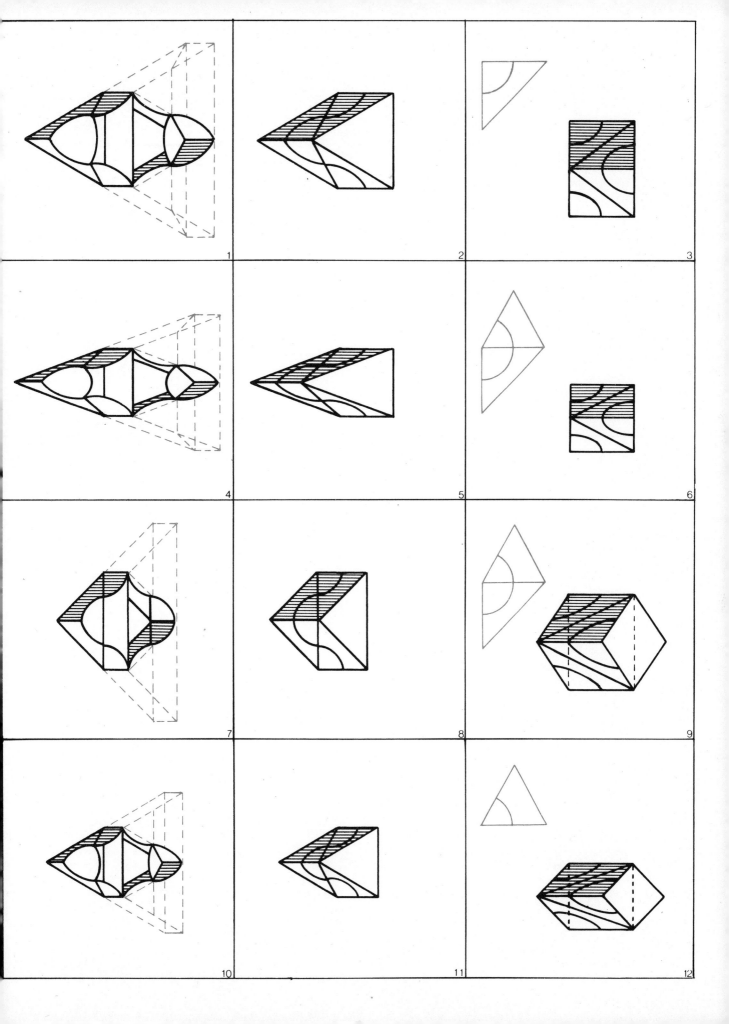

1

2

3

4

5

6

7

8

9

10

11

12

The process on the previous page has revealed a simple sub-structure which allows ordering of the expanding concept. On this page we see the partial integration of circle and square projected into three dimensions, relating cross-sectional 'thinking' to curved space. It is intended as an intermediary model between the rectilinear (post and lintel) and the curvilinear geometry more appropriate for today. The intention was to evolve systems which the non-specialist could understand (hence the cube as sub-structure) and manipulate with simple tools.

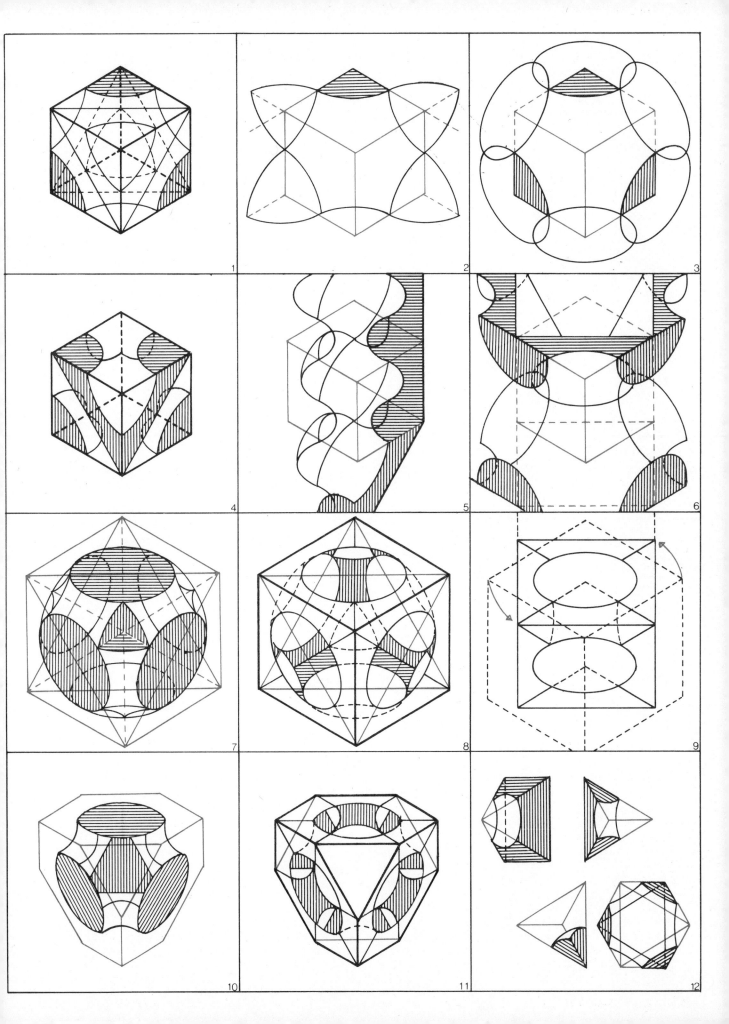

Illustrated opposite (fig. 1, fun-palace at Girvan, Scotland), is the elevation of a five-thousand-square-foot structure which was built in glass-fibre. In preparing drawings of these forms we found that the pattern on the paper was identical in both plan and elevation (this can be deduced from the elevation illustrated). Had we attempted to develop this idea on paper using only plan and elevation we would have been unsuccessful. We need three-dimensional models to develop these forms before they are reduced to a two-dimensional projection. The conceptual limitations of a 'simple' approach in the process are demonstrated by this example.

The structure illustrated employed only the curved shells of the cube family. If the units are solids then the services (electricity, water, etc.) are cored through each unit. One has the choice between facets (in blue) or curves (in black) both inside and outside the structure.

Figs. 2, 3 and 4 show the deformations of the cube which generated the forms. Beneath are demonstrated three of the methods of production: strips held in a lattice of cubes (fig. 5); a nest of positives (fig. 6) from which one removes the desired form and pours into the cavity the material required; a mould formed by the curved shell generated by pushing the two-dimensional cut-outs against a membrane. However, even the mould idea is too rigid for our needs. (Architecture is too often a mould for the life within, instead of vice versa.)

Fig. 8 demonstrates how the principle of deformation applied in figs. 2, 3, and 4 can be extended by squashing the cube to give greater flexibility in the curvature (fig. 9), and relating that deformed unit to the parent one (fig. 10).

1

2

3

4

5

6

7

8

9

10

Thus we move towards the possibility of exploiting our surroundings if we wish as directly as an artist or mathematician exploits his processes. But the structure on page 103 is still a very crude external model.

In order to be successful it has to be read as a pattern, leading the observer to a deeper understanding of the whole as a continuum. Practically, it must be capable of production by many methods and in a wide range of materials. It must move between the security bred of familiarity and a new security founded upon change; a truer security to be found in experiencing a sense of identity with the whole-in-motion as an active principle.

The motivation for this particular exercise was an awareness of the conceptual restrictions of the structures we inhabit and the physical rigidity of our present architecture. Architecture should be a true expression of a society's physical and conceptual structures if it is to house successfully and interact with the individuals of that society. If the architecture is seen as inappropriate or unsuccessful, then the answer may be in our whole approach to life, rather than the limited parameter of an industry or media.

These two structures fail because unlike the mosques they do not reflect the fluid nature of the continuum; they are 'frozen' concepts. They are really no more than pointers, like self-support systems (eco-houses), encouraging questioning of the *status quo*.

As we mentioned earlier, in connection with Islamic pattern, the stylistically unexpected can provide a shock to link with ideas already in the mind but overlaid by custom. But the innovator or revolutionary, in whatever sphere of human activity he is operating, may be no more able to perceive the whole context than the reactionary. The most successful revolutions are those with the most holistic approach; the ones which reflect awareness of fundamental patterns. But even these revolutions tend ultimately to fail in developing their original concepts. They are steadily modified by the larger processes of the whole and become mere currents in the stream of change.

We refer back to the exploiting of the construction lines, which in this context are movements or states of being. We are within the whole and thus are affecting the state. Thus subversion, rather than revolution, is closer to the evolutionary process, revealing orders that already exist in the movements of the whole. The most potent source of dynamic is the purposeful acquisition of knowledge, so it is within the ebb and flow of knowledge of the whole that we must operate. On other words, the new order, if it is to develop, must be a transformation of the old. While the fundamental structure barely alters, our viewing position may have to alter to give movement of shape and changes of scale.

We see on the top line of the diagram opposite an illusionary drawing of the cube (fig. 1), next the cube being twisted (fig. 2), and finally the half-twisted cube radically altering the original form to reveal new orders (fig. 3). As can be seen in fig. 2 it generates equilateral triangles with sides of the same length as the original cube, which incidentally can relate it to the previous cubic system. Fig. 3 is a plan view of the twisted cube (a dynamic pattern frequently seen on Islamic tiles).

The remainder of this page is a table describing the relationship of the cube drawings used in this chapter. On the top left-hand corner one face only can be seen (the square), while at the bottom right-hand corner is illustrated the hexagon. In fact the diagonal between these two points shows the phases of movement round the diagonal axis of the cube. The left-hand column shows the movement of the cube around a horizontal axis through two opposite faces, and the lower line describes the movement about an axis through the mid-points of two opposite edges. And so with three axes we can plot the intermediary movement of the cube and the pattern it forms in two dimensions. We can of course now exploit such a chart to understand the form of any related solid or curved shell inscribed within the cube. It is rewarding as a conceptual tool because of its movement which makes possible a large number of views in two dimensions with which we build our three-dimensional model.

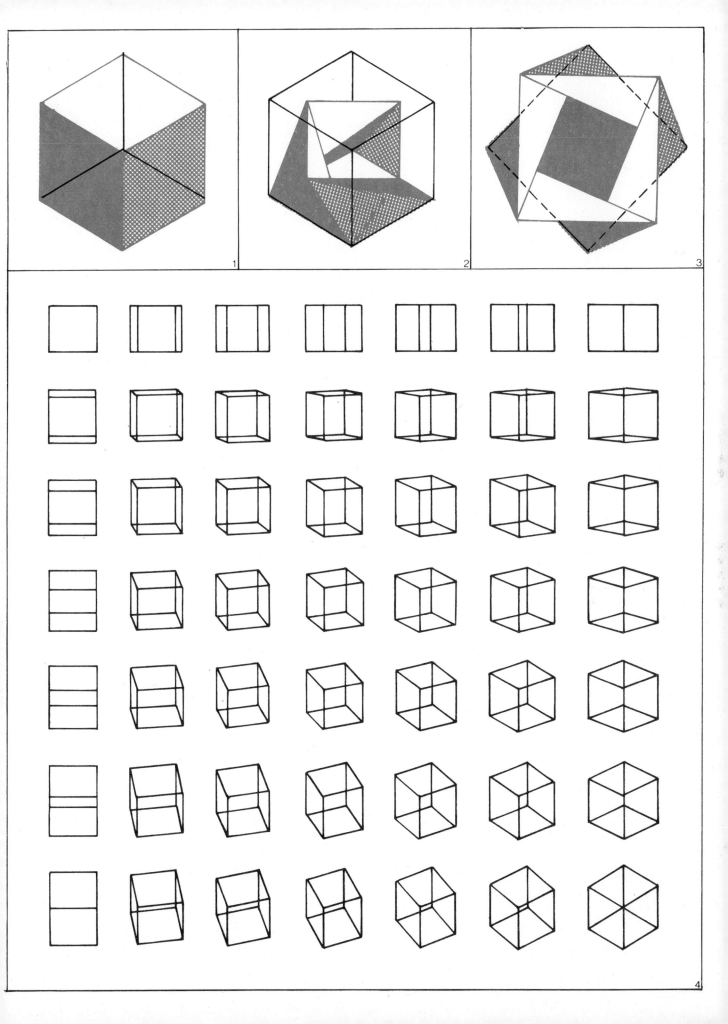

We have seen how the transition through the dimensions reveals layers of interrelated orders. Here we add an axial development by spinning the cube on three axes. We hang the cube on its diagonal axis, then begin the spin which leaves a trace (a blur) until a new form emerges (fig. 2). From the cube we have curved forms (parabolas) developed by the edges (fig. 3). The form is now like a cylinder, the parallel wires twisted to form negative curves (waisted forms) from zero curvature (cylindrical forms).

Fig. 4 (black) has superimposed (blue) two exposures of the cube in movement, forming a solid comprising two intersecting cubes with a shared diagonal axis. This model of two intersecting cubes is then spun on the axis through opposite edges and two views are drawn (figs. 5, 6). (Fig. 6 relates to fig. 3.)

We now make another model related to fig. 5 of two cubes with a shared axis through opposite edges but with a different time-lapse. We spin on this axis to generate (blue) one new form out of three (as in the last sequence). This in turn implies a third model (fig. 10) for the third axis, through opposite faces (see figs. 9 and 10). This is then spun revealing another new form from the three axes.

Thus a new order of forms is generated, all interrelating and as ambiguous in three dimensions as they are in two. This order generates only zero and negative curvature.

A stroboscopic effect gives us a striped pattern on the model, and we can control the width of the stripe by varying the speed of rotation. Thus with a static model of the mobile we can use striation to evoke a sense of a particular speed. Furthermore, when these models are constructed in wire we notice what appears to be a distinct three-dimensional form, which can be seen from numerous viewpoints, in the centre of the spinning wire cube. This shadow-form implies a positive curvature in the revolving cube. The size and the shape of the shadow depend on the speed of rotation. So we create with movement as our transformation agent a three-dimensional illusion which has no basis in matter. This is not merely a simple trace of a moving object, but an unexpected event.

When we explore other polyhedra under similar conditions it is interesting to note how difficult it is to predict the eventual shape in movement. In fact one can back-track to simple polygons and develop a deformation geometry of movement each with an independent system. To order in retrospect, and thus extend a generating system, we have used a two-dimensional table, but for these axial transformations a three-dimensional table would be required to induce the desired feedback. After a further transformation only a mobile grid would answer our need. Thus, parallel to the subject's transformation, the transformation of the ordering system in the external model must be maintained.

In a complex situation we must cast around for the most suitable process to harness for our ordering. The results will be dramatically affected (note the rapid expansion into 3D of data-handling methods), but as we have seen, the actual process of storage is an active one in which new relationships may be discovered. If there is a cumbersome black box between man and information the creative possibilities of observation of the ongoing process are limited.

The work of nineteenth-century mathematicians produced a totally fresh approach to, first, plane geometry, taking account of 'curved space'; second, the relativity of time; third, the implied expansion of the universe; and fourth, the 'intangibility' of matter. We are now in a world of frequencies, wave-lengths and resonance, an intangible energy field. The wave is our constant; fluctation is our pattern. Ideas such as these have accelerated man into a new cosmology, comprehension of which becomes increasingly difficult. Our extensors no longer involve us in experiments, but merely report results from this other-world of movement where concepts that we have always regarded as self-evident truths are turned upon their heads. (Yet within this cosmos of energy the simple hexagon is still apparent in the ordering of characteristics of the traces of field particles.)

The spin-off from these enquiries which are intangible at source appears all too tangible as technology. (Among our largest machines was one built to study the smallest phenomena known to man.) This prevents us from seeing the essential transience; only through this can we find the order that should underlie the conceptual expansion of man in the late twentieth century.

We still find the progression from zero to three dimensions, and the implications of their interrelationships in time, difficult; even more difficult are the predictive implications of any movement within that progression. The comprehension of four dimensions is nearly impossible but, by studying the pattern of development of the previous three dimensions, we predict something of the fourth and so stimulate fresh concepts.

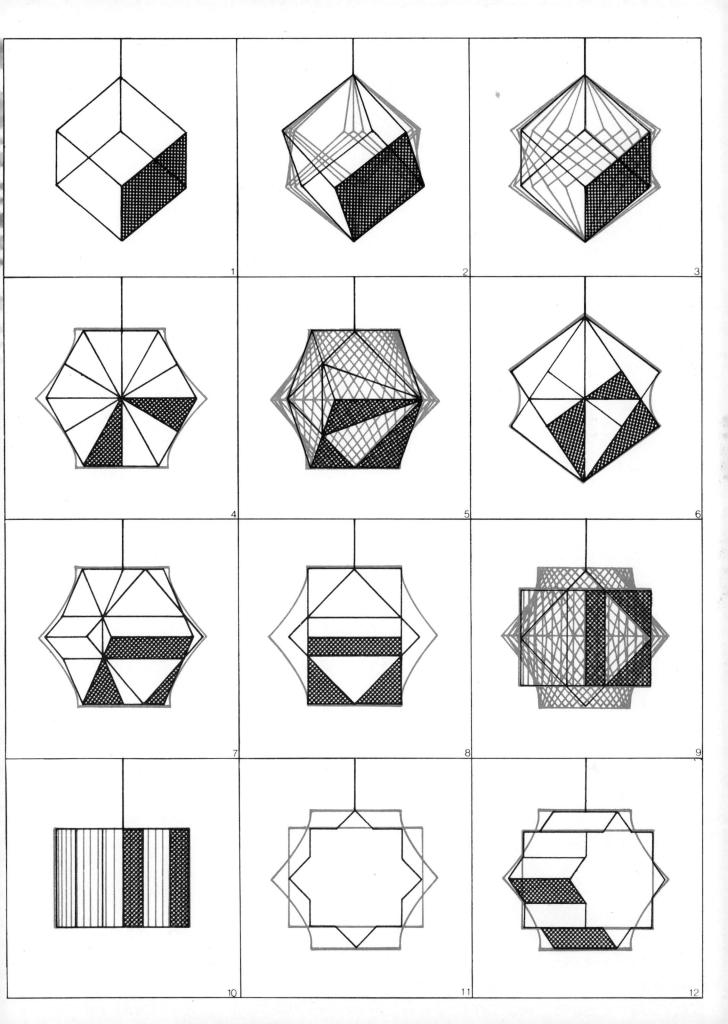

If we remind ourselves that we can understand each dimension only by reference to the previous one, then to understand four dimensions we should look to its three-dimensional cross-section. So we attempted to build in 3D a cross-section of a four-dimensional development of a cube. In order to make this even faintly comprehensible as a drawing, we revert to our knowledge of how we see three dimensions (that is, the synthesis of multiple viewpoints), and assemble on the two-dimensional page various views of this three-dimensional cross-section of a four-dimensional model. (This is the same as constructing in one dimension the experience of three dimensions.) We attempt it because the most interesting aspect is not the successful, or unsuccessful, communication of the idea of 4D, but the strange assemblage of *many* illusionary figures which now occurs. These figures appear to have little relationship to each other, but in fact are different views of the same three-dimensional projection. The resulting assemblage in our internal model may not, on this evidence, be much use for building the cross-section of a specific four-dimensional figure, but it does express the mobility of these developments through the dimensions, and perhaps as a result it is more relevant as an example of the role of illusionary models in holistic concepts. The feed-back now transforms our experience of pattern and we can use the simplest process to generate conceptual developments.

We can see in this drawing confirmation of relationships not seen in lower dimensions. But here they are relationships within the same object. It is now more readily understandable why certain configurations fascinate us, holding our attention. To unlock the shape's potential we need the knowledge of dimensional development (that is, development through time and space).

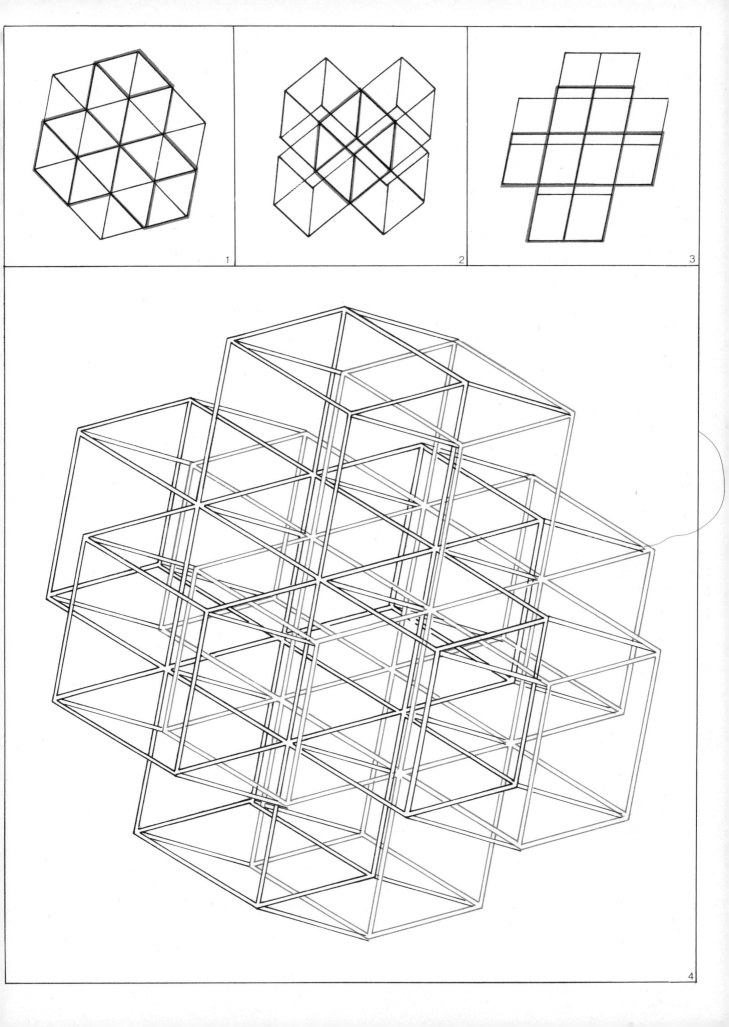

1

2

3

4

6 A Way of Thinking

Throughout this book we have been discussing illusion as a means of transforming a process (to alter or expand a concept) by revealing alternatives through the mechanics of ambiguity in perception. We have also examined briefly a culture in which a way of thinking generated astonishing concepts and in which the arts and sciences were inseparable. Through the reworking of Islamic pattern we became convinced that modern art and design had more to offer in creating a visual language relevant to modern cosmology than they were at present offering.

An array of illusionary techniques enables an artist to create working models which, by implication, reveal something of our understanding of the world about us. This understanding is of a qualitative character. An involvement beyond mere passive experience is required if art is to be significant communication. The abstract artist requires as incisive and tough an approach as the mathematician who, through examining his experience of mathematics, being aware of pattern and structure, and with an exploratory motivation similar to that of the artist, makes comprehensible the extension of that process.

Fine art and mathematics apply themselves to extending their language to order and relate, and hence extend, the shifting visual and intellectual intuitive concepts of our time (mathematics by quantifying, art by 'qualitifying'). Yet to link the two disciplines is misleading, since the twentieth-century artist has made his research, not a means to an end, but an end in itself. The fine arts are rarely seen as being as necessary as mathematics, and at best the artist receives premature enshrinement when his works (by-products of processes) are separated from life as collectors' pieces.

It is hardly surprising therefore that the arts are in a defensive position, abdicating from the main stream of their disciplines of application. They are now within a quantifying and analytical rather than a synthetic society. Art has become so individualized that the commonly-accepted structures required for communication are almost precluded. There must shortly be a true re-appraisal — not just of the role of the artist, as this is merely a symptom of the need for a renascence of synthetic thinking — but a renewal of toughness in structuring, and a renewed discipline of education. If we fail to achieve this renewal, a cultural dark age will surely be upon us. How can we hope to avoid this fate?

First, we have seen we need a goal that is ultimately unattainable. That goal we have described as whole-sense. Full knowledge of the whole is clearly impossible, yet it is only with this 'whole-sense' that any part is effectively comprehensible. A growing awareness of a holistic pattern is the most productive social governor, the possible basis of a philosophy of education, and a realistic device to avoid codification.

Second, we must move towards the goal by a way of thinking which can be described as 'intellectual intuition'. Intellectual intuition is both active and passive, objective and subjective; it merely re-combines what we have unsuccessfully attempted to separate. That whole-sense would then modify hierarchical divisions, integrating different levels of society, avoiding reductionist answers and operating a constant, never wholly definable hypothesis.

Intellectual intuition combines the processes of the internal and external models of an illusionary reality, undergoing a constant transformation which is only comprehensible with the use of pattern.

Patterns structure our thinking, i.e. pattern is the 'structure of mind', therefore to evolve our knowledge of pattern is also to evolve ourselves. We are apparently moving again into a visually orientated period from a long verbal tradition and are therefore woefully inept at 'seeing' our situation clearly. The need is for the interpenetration of both elements within our thought processes. This implies a much deeper understanding of both structures and their relation to the whole. At present little is being achieved in the visual field to make possible an integrative approach. We need a feeling for pattern if we are to understand more fully the programmes which will enable us to build a model continuum to generate more fruitfully than our present internal model-making procedures will allow. It will still require the concept of 'model', as all 'facts' are subjective — that is, affected by the structure of the mind receiving those facts. We can only know what we are physically capable of knowing — ultimately the mind cannot know its simultaneous self. A fundamental conceptual pattern must be abstracted from the ever-changing view of reality to allow smooth transformations to take place under the pressure of new data. In this way we can perhaps avoid the trauma of total re-appraisal which results when the overall pattern goes unrecognized. If we are aware of the integrative pattern of experience, and our involvement in the basic rhythms of being, we may begin to maximize our potential controlling or exploiting even of those aspects of our psycho-physical selves which we have yet fully to examine.

This integrative pattern is now within our current cosmology, a scaleless, multi-dimensional continuum, seen as complex, appearing almost random, often sensed rather than known, a projection of our common experience (knowledge). It is rewarding only in so far as we are able to be aware of our involvement in it — to understand and therefore to order and thus give meaning, through a way of thinking, to the dynamic pattern of our existence.

Further Reading

The publications below are grouped in relation to the main threads of the argument within this book.

Islamic Art, Architecture and Philosophy

EDWARDS, A. Cecil	*The Persian Carpet*, London 1953
GRUBE, Ernest J	*World of Islam*, London 1966
HILL, Derek and GRABAR, Oleg	*Islamic Architecture and its Decoration*, London 1964
HOAG, John D.	*Western Islamic Architecture*, London 1963
KYBALOVA, L. and DARBOIS, D.	*Carpets of the Orient*, London 1969
MORRIS, James, WOOD, Roger and WRIGHT, Denis	*Persia*, London 1969
NASR, S. H.	*Introduction to Islamic Cosmological Doctrines*, Cambridge, Mass., 1964
PINDER-WILSON, R.	*Islamic Art*, London 1957
PIZZINELLI, J. Luigi Mario	*The Life and Time of Mohammed*, London 1968
POPE, Arthur Upham	*Persian Architecture*, London 1965
————	*Survey of Persian Art* (Vol. XIV), Proceedings from 4th Congress Persian Art, Asia Institute, 1960
RICE, David Talbot	*Islamic Art*, London 1965
SEHERR-THOSS, S. and H.	*Design and Color in Islamic Architecture*, Washington 1968
VOGT-GOKNIL, U.	*Living Architecture — Ottoman*, London 1966
VOLWAHSEN, A.	*Living Architecture — Islamic Indian*, London 1970
WHEELER, Mortimer	*World Architecture — Splendours of the East*, London 1965
WILBER, D.	*Persian Gardens and Garden Pavilions*, Tokyo 1962

Psychology and Physiology of Perception with Reference to Art

ATTEAVE, F.	'Multistability in Perception', *Scientific American*, December 1971
CLERK, W. Le Gros	'Sensory Experience and Brain Structure' — 32nd Maudsley Lecture, *Journal of Mental Science* (Vol. 104) January 1958. Royal Medico-psychological Association, London 1958
DE BONO, E.	*The Mechanism of Mind*, London 1969
FRASER STEELE, G.	*Brain, Mind and Consciousness*, London 1958
GESCHWIND, N.	'Language and the Brain', *Scientific American*, April 1972
GOMBRICH, E. H.	'The Visual Image', *Scientific American*, September 1972
————	*Art and Illusion*, London 1960
GREGORY, R. L.	*The Intelligent Eye*, London 1970
————	*Eye and Brain*, London 1966
LUCKIESH, M.	*Visual Illusions*, London 1965
PETTIGREW, J.	'The Neurophysiology of Binocular Vision', *Scientific American*, August 1972

Mathematics

COXETER, H. S. M.	*Regular Polytopes*, New York 1963
CRITCHLOW, K.	*Order in Space*, London 1969
CUNDY, H. M. and ROLLET, A. P.	*Mathematical Models* (2nd ed.), Oxford 1951
D'ARCY THOMPSON, W.	*On Growth and Form* (abridged ed.), Cambridge 1961
FREEBURY, H. A.	*History of Mathematics*, London 1960
GARDNER, M.	*Mathematical Puzzles and Diversions*, London 1961
————	*More Mathematical Puzzles and Diversions*, London 1963
KEPES, Gyorgy	*Module, Symmetry and Proportion*, London 1960
KLINE, Morris	*Mathematics in Western Culture*, London 1954
————	*Mathematics in the Modern World* (*Readings from 'Scientific American'*), London 1968
MESSICK, D.	*Mathematical Thinking in the Behavioural Sciences* (*Readings from 'Scientific American'*), London 1968
PEDOE, D.	*The Gentle Art of Mathematics*, London 1958
PHILLIPS, F. C.	*An Introduction to Crystallography*, Edinburgh 1971
SOLOMON, C.	*Mathematics*, London 1969